A New Owner's
Guide to
WEST HIGHLAND
WHITE TERRIERS

JG-116

Overleaf: Adult and puppy Westies owned by Joanne and Jaimi Glodek.

Opposite page: Ch. Hayastan Highland King, CD, SE, owned by Lou Herczeg and Dawn Martin.

The Publisher wishes to acknowledge the following owners of the dogs in this book: Mitzi Beals, Stephanie Capkovic, Dawn F. Diemer, Dorothy Grocott, Lou Herczeg, Thom and Amy Juzwik, Ida and Joseph Keushgenian, Rita M. Kline, E. Sue Loyall, Patti Marks, Dawn Martin, Kathleen E. May, Marian Moeller, Bob and Winnie Napoli, Allison Platt, Geraldine Sedora, Lynne A. Sedotto, Kathleen Spradleg, Barbara Stiles, Lynn Stonesifer, Rolanda Sturtevans, Pat Sullivan, Timberlane Kennels.

Photographers: John Ashbey, 4U2C Photography, Isabelle Francais, Chet Jezierski, Robert Pearcy, Ron Reagan, Vince Serbin, Alex Smith Photography, Karen J. Taylor.

The author acknowledges the contribution of Judy Iby of the following chapters: Sport of Purebred Dogs, Identification and Finding the Lost Dog, Traveling with Your Dog, Health Care, Behavior and Canine Communication.

T.F.H. Publications, Inc.
One TFH Plaza
Third and Union Avenues
Neptune City, NJ 07753

05 06 07 08 09 3 5 7 9 8 6 4

This book has been published with the intent to provide accurate and authoritative information in regard to the subject matter within. While every precaution has been taken in preparation of this book, the publisher and author assume no responsibility for errors or omissions. Neither is any liability assumed for damages resulting from the use of the information herein.

ISBN 0-7938-2765-5

A New Owner's Guide to
WEST HIGHLAND WHITE TERRIERS

Dawn Martin

Contents

An energetic Westie pup is always on the go!

The typical round-faced look of a well-groomed Westie.

A Westie pup needs Nylafloss® for good dental health.

Agility is just one activity in which Westies excel.

This Westie is "sitting pretty."

ORIGIN of the West Highland White Terrier

Although the exact origin of the West Highland White Terrier is shrouded in mystery and lost to time, there is sufficient evidence to indicate that the breed is several hundred years old. Both written and pictorial accounts exist as far back as the early 17th century. It is told and retold that James I of England (1566-1625) sent a request to Argyllshire for six little white "earthe dogges," which were to have been presented as a gift to the King of France.

In 1839, Sir Edwin Landseer painted the now famous work entitled *Dignity and Impudence*. It

Dignity and Impudence was painted by Sir Edward Landseer in 1839. This print is part of the author's collection while the original hangs in the National Gallery in London.

shows a Westie lying side-by-side with the master's hound looking out at the world from a dog coop. Landseer was an artist of note, and there can be no doubt that this quizzical, dark-eyed dog is indeed an early highlander.

Throughout the 19th century, the Westie was known by various names including White Scotch, Little Skye, Cairn, Roseneath, and Poltalloch Terrier. This makes for added confusion when reviewing written accounts in early dog related books and publications.

Col. E.D. Malcolm of Poltalloch is credited with the development of the West Highland White Terrier as we know the breed today. Due to his earlier efforts to exhibit at shows at the

An early illustration of a Scottish Terrier and Skye Terrier. The Westie was known by these and other names throughout the 19th century.

turn of the century, a small group of enthusiasts joined together to create a club. Col. Malcolm's love for the breed and its future is evident in the selection of the name West Highland White Terrier. By discarding the commonly used names of Roseneath or Poltalloch Terrier, he ensured that all white earth dogs of the western coast of Scotland would be included. This unselfish act led to the strengthening and uniting of the breed.

In October 1904, classes for the West Highland White Terrier were offered at the annual show of the Scottish Kennel Club in Edinburgh.

The breed was first shown as the Roseneath Terrier in the United States in 1906 at the Westminster Kennel Club in New York City. It was not until 1909 that the name was changed to West Highland White Terrier and the national club was recognized by the American Kennel Club.

The West Highland White Terrier's heritage lies in the rocky, rugged terrain of Scotland's west coast region.

HERITAGE

The name terrier is a form of the Latin word "terra," which means earth. By virtue of their name, terriers, as a group, were derived from hard working earth dogs. Because of the rugged mountains and rocky terrain, travel was severely limited. This led to the creation of local varieties or strains to which there was little or no outcrossing for many generations. Embodied in the terriers is a keen hunting instinct still present today.

The highlander owes its heritage to the west coast region of Scotland. Therein lies the key to its basic personality. Hunting in between the rocks and caverns after fox, badgers, or otters required strength, intelligence and perseverance in the face of adversaries.

Hunting among the rocks and in caverns required a hard-working dog with keen instinct, intelligence, and endurance.

A terrier that was hesitant or lacked the ability to kill or drive the foe from its den would not have survived the grueling battle beneath the earth. Few tears were shed over the loss of such a poor worker.

STANDARD for the West Highland White Terrier

A breed standard is the criterion by which the appearance (and to a certain extent, the temperament as well) of any given dog is made subject to objective measurement. Basically, the standard for any breed is a definition of the perfect dog, to which all specimens of the breed are compared. Breed standards are always subject to change through review by the national breed club for each dog, so it is always wise to keep up with developments in a breed by checking the publications of your national kennel club.

The overall appearance of a Westie is that of a hardy, alert-looking terrier with a white, neatly trimmed coat that is left longer around the face.

OFFICIAL AKC STANDARD FOR THE WEST HIGHLAND WHITE TERRIER

General Appearance—The West Highland White Terrier is a small, game, well-balanced hardy looking terrier, exhibiting good showmanship, possessed with no small amount of self-esteem, strongly built, deep in chest and back ribs, with a straight back and powerful hindquarters on muscular legs, and exhibiting in marked degree a great combination of strength and activity. The coat is about two inches long, white in color, hard, with plenty of soft undercoat. The dog should be neatly presented, the longer coat on the back and sides, trimmed to blend into the shorter neck and shoulder coat. Considerable hair is left around the head to act as a frame for the face to yield a typical Westie expression.

Size, Proportion, Substance—The ideal size is eleven inches at the withers for dogs and ten inches for bitches. A slight deviation is acceptable. The Westie is a compact dog, with good balance and substance. The body between the withers and the root of the tail is slightly shorter than the height at the withers. Short-coupled and well boned. *Faults—*Over or under height limits. Fine boned.

Head—Shaped to present a round appearance from the

front. Should be in proportion to the body. *Expression—*
Piercing, inquisitive, pert. *Eyes—*Widely set apart, medium in
size, almond shaped, dark brown in color, deep set, sharp and
intelligent. Looking from under heavy eyebrows, they give a
piercing look. Eye rims are black. *Faults—*Small, full or light
colored eyes. *Ears—*Small, carried tightly erect, set wide apart,
on top outer edge of the skull. They terminate in a sharp point,
and must never be cropped. The hair on the ears is trimmed
short and is smooth and velvety, free of fringe at the tips. Black
skin pigmentation is preferred. *Faults—*Round-pointed, broad,
large ears set closely together, not held tightly erect, or placed
too low on the side of the head.

Skull—Broad, slightly longer than the muzzle, not flat on top
but slightly domed between the ears. It gradually tapers to the
eyes. There is a defined stop, eyebrows are heavy. *Faults—*
Long or narrow skull. *Muzzle—*Blunt, slightly shorter than
skull, powerful and gradually tapering to the nose, which is
large and black. The jaws are level and powerful. Lip pigment
is black. *Faults—*Muzzle longer than skull. Nose color other
than black. *Bite—*The teeth are large for the size of the dog.
There must be six incisor teeth between the canines of both
lower and upper jaws. An occasional missing premolar is
acceptable. *Faults—*Teeth defective or misaligned. Any
incisors missing or several premolars missing. Teeth overshot
or undershot.

Neck, Topline, Body—*Neck—*Muscular and well set on
sloping shoulders. The length of neck should be in proportion
to the remainder of the dog. *Faults—*Neck too long or too

*The Westie's
hair is
shaped
around the
face to give
the head a
round
appearance,
and the head
should be in
proportion to
the body.*

short. ***Topline***—Flat and level, both standing and moving. ***Faults***—High rear, any deviation from above. ***Body***—Compact and of good substance. Ribs deep and well arched in the upper half of rib, extending at least to the elbows, and presenting a flattish side appearance. Back ribs of considerable depth, and distance from last rib to upper thigh as short as compatible with free movement of the body. Chest very deep and extending to the elbows, with breadth in proportion to the size of the dog. Loin short, broad and strong. ***Faults***—Back

The Westie should possess a flat, level topline. His tail is somewhat short and carrot-shaped, and, when held erect, should not extend higher than the top of the skull.

In a young Westie, the ear-set can be seen clearly. The ears are carried erect and set wide apart on the top outer edges of the skull.

weak, either too long or too short. Barrel ribs, ribs above elbows. *Tail*—Relatively short, with good substance, and shaped like a carrot. When standing erect it is never extended above the top of the skull. It is covered with hard hair without feather, as straight as possible, carried gaily but not curled over the back. The tail is set on high enough to that the spine does not slope down to it. The tail is never docked. *Faults*—Set too low, long, thin, carried at half-mast, or curled over back.

The strength and endurance that the Westie was originally bred for is apparent in the muscularity of his short legs.

Forequarters— *Angulation, Shoulders*—Shoulder blades are well laid back and well knit at the backbone. The shoulder blade should attach to an upper arm of moderate length, and sufficient angle to allow for definite body overhang. *Faults*— Steep or loaded shoulders. Upper arm too short or too straight. *Legs*— Forelegs are muscular and well boned, relatively short, but with sufficient length to set the dog up so as not to be too close to the ground. The legs are reasonably straight, and thickly covered with short, hard hair. They are set in under the shoulder blades with definite body overhang before them. Height from elbow to withers and elbow to ground should be approximately the same. *Faults*—Out at elbows, light bone, fiddle-front. *Feet*—Forefeet are larger than the hind ones, are round, proportionate in size, strong, thickly padded; they may properly be turned out slightly. Dewclaws may be removed. Black pigmentation is most desirable on pads of all feet and nails, although nails may lose coloration in older dogs.

A breed standard is a set of traits that ideal representatives of the breed should possess. A dog must closely resemble the standard to fare well in conformation showing.

Hindquarters— *Angulation*—Thighs are very muscular, well angulated, not set wide apart, with hock well bent, short and parallel when viewed from the rear. *Legs*— Rear legs are muscular and relatively short and sinewy. *Faults*—Weak hocks, long hocks, lack of angulation.

Cowhocks. **Feet**—Hind feet are smaller than front feet, and are thickly padded. Dewclaws may be removed.

Coat—Very important and seldom seen to perfection. Must be double-coated. The head is shaped by plucking the hair, to present the round appearance. The outer coat consists of straight hard white hair, about two inches long, with shorter coat on neck and shoulders, properly blended and trimmed to blend shorter areas into furnishings, which are longer on stomach and legs. The ideal coat is hard, straight and white, but a hard straight coat which may have some wheaten tipping is preferable to a white fluffy or soft coat. **Faults**—Soft coat. Any silkiness or tendency to curl. Any open or single coat, or one which is too short.

Indy, Ava, Amelia, and Alexis are four beautiful Westies. Breeders use the standard as a guideline to help them consistently produce top-quality dogs.

Color—The color is white, as defined by the breed's name. **Faults**—Any coat color other than white. Heavy wheaten color.

Gait—Free, straight and easy all around. It is a distinctive gait, not stilted, but powerful, with reach and drive. In front the leg is freely extended forward by the shoulder. When seen from the front the legs do not move square, but tend to move toward the center of gravity. The hind movement is free, strong and fairly close. The hocks are freely flexed and drawn close under the body, so that when moving off the foot the body is thrown or pushed forward with some force. Overall ability to move is usually best evaluated from the side, and topline remains level. **Faults**—Lack of reach in front, and/or drive behind. Stiff, stilted or too wide movement.

Temperament—Alert, gay, courageous and self-reliant, but friendly. **Faults**—Excess timidity or excess pugnacity.

A dog's movement is evaluated in the show ring. A Westie's gait should appear straight, powerful, and easy.

LIVING with a Westie

Today's West Highland White Terriers differ little in personality from their working ancestors. They are highly intelligent, game, inquisitive, busy dogs — a lot of dog in a small package. They should never be confused with or compared to such lap dog breeds as the Maltese or the Bichon Frise. Nor are they like small children in fur coats. They are terriers, still retaining all their natural keen hunting instincts, and should be reared with respect to their canine needs.

The intelligent, inquisitive personality of today's Westie closely resembles that of his working ancestors.

Parameters and basic training are necessary elements should you choose to have a West Highland White Terrier live in your home. An untrained Westie

18

Your Westie's idea of acceptable behavior is probably a lot different from yours. Basic training is necessary and should begin as soon as you bring your Westie pup home.

will soon make its own rules and allow *you* to live by them.

The dog's mind matures slowly as many Westie owners can attest. Destructive puppy behaviors often last until two years of age. One safeguard against such household destruction is a crate. There are many advantages to using such a device for your puppy and adolescent dog.

1. A properly crate-trained Westie is a happy, well adjusted, secure dog who knows his place among his human counterparts. He has a positive outlook and is always willing to follow and join in family activities.

2. By nature, all dogs are den dwellers and creatures of habit. It is the number one reason they are so easily housebroken. They will not soil where they eat and sleep. A crate offers your dog just that, a den of his own. A castle, so to speak, where he is king of his den.

3. A crate is his home away from home. While at the

groomers, he is relaxed and content waiting in a crate for your anticipated return. Also, veterinarian hospital stays for neutering or sickness are met with the security of a crate. In addition, should kennel boarding or travel become a part of his life, a Westie who has learned to eat in his crate will continue to do so while away from home.

Basic training should begin the day you bring your Westie home. Avoid making the common error of giving your newcomer too much freedom and then changing the rules a few months later. This is not only confusing, but often leads to a breakdown in your ability to properly communicate with your dog.

By nature, all dogs are pack animals. A pack consists of one alpha, or top dog, and a descending order of rank among the remaining members. A dog's perception and approach to life is very simple and honest. Therefore, the ideal top dog should be confident and loving with well-established rules and boundaries.

Today's Westie needs just that in his human pack leader. Once clearly defined rules are established, your dog will be set for life. Starting off right from the beginning is imperative. Do not delay in becoming the alpha or top dog.

Puppies can and will do the most amusing things. Puppy barking can be quite amusing. They will jump, pounce, and bark incessantly at a small bug or toy. Now is the time to teach the "that's enough" command. While the puppy is in the act of barking, startle him by shaking a metal can containing a few stones or pennies as you give the

The innocent puppy look isn't going to work this time—it's quite obvious that curious Cassidy has been "investigating" something.

command "that's enough." The moment your Westie pup stops and looks toward you, praise him with a "Good boy. What a good puppy." Give him a new toy or remove him from the area that is causing him to bark. The object is for him to learn "that's enough" by getting it right. Brief bouts of barking while playing or encountering a new situation should be ignored. Continued barking needs to be dealt with promptly.

Just like most youngsters, energetic Westie pups love to play! "Tonya" and "Nancy" are typical playful pups.

A promising "pack" of Westie pups sired by Ch. Hayastan's Magic Moment out of Ch. Dawn's Kop N' A Plea, SE.

Take care when choosing what will and what will not be accepted when your Westie becomes an adult. Remember, avoid changing the rules. This only leads to confusion and a breakdown in communication.

SELECTING a Westie

So you think a Westie is the right breed of dog for you and your family. Before you rush out and buy the first one that comes along, stop and think. Westies live approximately 13 years. The novelty of a new puppy quickly wears off for children and the daily routine and maintenance will be the parent's responsibility. Do you have the time? Do you really want a dog? Lucky is the Westie who is wanted by the whole family.

LOCATING A BREEDER

There are several ways to locate a breeder. Contact the American Kennel Club at 1-900-AKC- PUPS. Request the name and address of the secretary of the West Highland White Terrier Club of America. The National Club secretary can provide a listing of breeders in your geographic area. Many all-breed dog clubs offer a puppy referral service. Their phone numbers can be obtained by calling your local humane shelter. Attend a dog show. This is an ideal way to meet the breeders and their dogs face to face.

Start your inquiries well in advance. It may take a while to find the right breeder. A reputable breeder should be a person with a good working knowledge of the breed. He should be willing and able to answer your questions and concerns about the purchase of a Westie. He should be a person you can trust and rely on to guide you in your quest for the right puppy.

While you are accumulating breeders' names in your area, make

Where were the puppies born? Where are they kept as they are being raised? These are just two of the important questions you should ask when searching for a breeder.

A well-adjusted Westie pup should get along with his littermates. The puppy's socialization is something you should ask the breeder about.

a list of questions you feel are important regarding how they raise their pups. Examples include, but are not limited to, the following:

1. Where are the puppies born and raised (house, kennel, inside, outside, etc.)

2. At what age are they ready to leave (9–12 weeks, etc.)?

3. What shots will they have had? Who gives the shots (breeder, veterinarian, etc.)?

4. Will they be veterinarian checked? How many times? Health certified?

5. Do they offer a health guarantee?

6. Are the pups crate trained before leaving the breeder? (this is a big plus.)

7. Are the puppies good with children?

8. Are the pups socialized? How? Where? To what?

9. When are they planning a litter?

10. Are they available to answer questions should the

need arise two months, one year, three years, etc., from now?

Make a chart and keep track of what breeders have to offer. When you find several you like, make an appointment, be considerate and call to cancel, if necessary. While you are there, don't be afraid to ask questions, but do keep in mind that a good breeder will be interviewing you in return. Some questions a breeder might ask you are:

1. Have you owned a dog before? What kind?
2. Is your yard fenced? Are you planning to put up a fence?
3. Will the puppy be shown, bred or neutered?
4. Do you have children? Ages?
5. Do you work? Have you made arrangements for housetraining?
6. What do you want and expect from a Westie in terms of temperament?

CHOOSING THE RIGHT PUPPY

Choosing the right puppy for you is a serious decision. The dog's basic temperament must fit your personality and family lifestyle.

A high energy puppy will not fare well in an apartment and may be an inappropriate choice for an elderly couple. Whereas, a quiet, noise-sensitive puppy would be a disaster for a busy household with small children. The time spent selecting the appropriate puppy will be paid back many times over the course of the dog's lifetime.

Learn to be observant when viewing parents and puppies. Many breeders color code their puppies at birth with different colors of nail polish. This makes for easy identification of each individual at a glance. Temperament is inherited. What you see in a parent or other adult relatives in the household may be what you end up with in a puppy. Are the adults happy, outgoing and friendly? Are they active or quiet? If you do not like the temperament of the adults, don't buy the puppy. All puppies are cute, but you would be wise to see the parents first.

You may find some breeders who do puppy temperament testing. The test is performed at seven weeks of age before the pups enter the fear stage. They are tested individually in an unfamiliar area by an experienced tester. It is best if they have not met the tester before. There are a series of tests that are performed in a preset order. When combined, they give a personality profile of the pup's basic temperament.

Bear in mind that there are no passes or fails in the test. A puppy cannot flunk a temperament test. It is not uncommon for a breeder to suggest or determine which pup or puppies may suit your needs. Therefore, the more a breeder knows about you and your family, the better able he is to pick the right puppy for you. Remember, a knowledgeable breeder is your key to selecting the right puppy.

Fear Period: Eight to Ten Weeks

All puppies enter a "fear flight" stage at eight weeks of age. This stage lasts approximately two weeks. In the wild, this is a natural defense for all young animals. It is a time when they become aware and distrustful of their environment.

A litter of "color-coded" Westie pups. Breeders will often mark their pups with nail polish so that each individual can be easily identified.

Puppies at this stage in their lives must be handled with care. Any bad

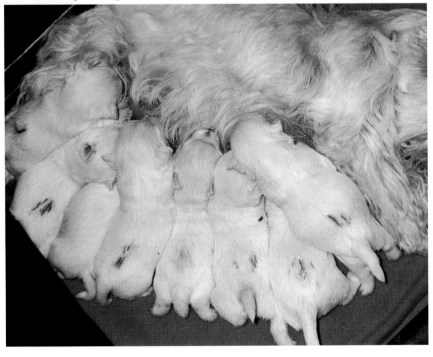

experiences will be forever imprinted in their minds. If you are visiting with pups at this time in their young lives, do take care not to startle or scare them. Avoid loud noises or quick moves.

Group Observation

To begin your own evaluation, the pups should be viewed first as a group and then individually. Ask the breeder to confine the pups in an area where you may quietly observe them. Ideally, they should not know you are there (example: outside in a secure pen while you watch from the window). Many things can be told from passive observation.

Energy Level The choice of the correct energy level puppy for your household is of chief importance. You must determine what you want from an adult dog. Are you an active

The seemingly endless exuberance of a high-energy pup can be quite amusing to watch. This type of pup will require a lot of exercise and much attenton from his owner.

person? Do you hike or take long walks? Will the dog be included? This requires a good energy level and stamina. Do you live in an apartment or high-rise in a city? This would require a lower energy dog who will not become frustrated and destructive by lack of activity.

Energy Levels Can vary greatly in the same litter. Some pups will bound and jump from one thing to the next while others are content to play quietly with a toy or littermate. Keep your needs in mind as you watch them interact. The higher energy active pups are amusing to watch. Do bear in mind they will require plenty of regular exercise all through their lives. This dog can become destructive and unhappy if confined or left alone for long periods of time. It is best for the high energy puppy to have a secure fenced yard. Walking is usually not enough. The quieter littermate who is content to play with a toy by himself would be a wiser choice for a working household.

So much to do, so little time! High energy Westies will often bound from one thing to the next in search of something new.

Dominant Personality Depending on the number in the litter, one or two pups will remain on top of every situation. They appear to be the leaders. They may climb on the backs of littermates, steal toys at will and stand rigidly on their toes with tail up and ears alert.

The dominant pup will need a strong human leader and is often not a good choice for the first-time dog owner or families with young children. Do not confuse dominance with activity levels. A quiet puppy can be dominant and self assured with a lower energy level.

Busybody A busybody puppy is carefree in attitude with a medium to high energy level. This type plays readily with toys, any toy, and gives them up quickly to littermates. He is often dominated by other littermates but does not appear to care. This puppy's happy-go-lucky personality makes him an ideal choice for a family with children. He likes to be included and will play with children without the need to dominate.

Shy or Noise Sensitive This puppy avoids confrontation. He can usually be found sitting transfixed in a corner of the play area watching, but not participating. Activity, noise and his littermates overwhelm him.

This puppy in particular needs to be looked at by himself. When removed from his siblings, this quiet pup will blossom and glow. Oftentimes he is the sweetest and most cuddly of all the pups. He will make an ideal pet for a quiet, sedate family. Unlike his boisterous littermates, his desire to avoid confrontation makes him easy to train.

This young Westie has an attitude! Jumping up and trying to lick, paw, or bite a person's fingers are ways that a dominant puppy will show his personality.

Noise sensitive puppies and young children are not a winning combination. Improperly placed in a busy household with noisy, active children often spells disaster. When unable to handle the everyday stress, this puppy can become a fear biter.

Individual Observation

After carefully observing the litter as a group, have the breeder bring one up at a time into the room. A puppy likes to explore, so let him. Do not immediately grab, hold, restrain, or try to control him in any way. If possible, sit quietly on the floor and let him discover you.

Energy Level This is easily assessed by noting how active the pup is after a few minutes in the room. Does he run around constantly while exploring? This is indicative of a high energy level. Medium level pups mostly trot or walk and occasionally run. Low energy pups usually sit and observe or play quietly.

Dominant Personality The dominant pup has a cock of the walk attitude and is very independent. His tail is never down. Should he choose to visit you on the floor, he will do so by placing his front feet on you. He may paw, lick, or bite your fingers. He can come in any energy level and care should be taken not to confuse a low energy level dominant pup with a shy pup.

Busybody A busybody is easy to spot. He likes to meet everyone and loves attention. As he approaches you, his tail drops slightly and wags quickly from side to side. He often rolls

over wiggling while exposing his stomach. He is never dominant and does not wish to be.

Shy Pup This pup approaches people, toys, and every new situation with caution. His legs are usually bent into a crouching position and his tail is usually held low. Once he is convinced you are not a threat, he will cuddle by you and gently wag his tail. The shy pup does not jump at you or nip at fingers. He is a gentle soul.

Noise Sensitive From daily observation, a breeder is better equipped to determine which pups, if any, are noise sensitive. Thankfully, due to their working ancestry, few Westies are noise sensitive. An underground working terrier was required to meet his foe face-to-face. A Westie who was noise sensitive would have failed at the challenge of a growling, snapping, screeching fox or badger. Therefore, in years past, it would have been eliminated from the breeding pool. The occasional exception should not be placed with small children and should never be bred.

Retrieving After the pup has had time to settle down in the room with you and your family, try crumpling a small piece of paper into a ball. He should become interested as the paper makes noise. While he's looking, toss it out about 4 to 6 feet in front of you. Make sure he sees it. Wait quietly as he approaches the paper. When he gets to it, begin to call softly and encourage him to return with it to you.

Not all Westie puppies retrieve at a young age. One who goes out to the paper and then returns without it will often become a retriever later. A retrieving puppy is a good choice

A shy pup approaches everything with caution. He likes to thoroughly investigate any new situation until he is satisfied that it will not pose a threat.

for a family with children. He is usually more adaptable and willing to please.

The Older Dog

If work schedules make it impossible to come home midday or you do not want the chore of raising a young puppy, consider the purchase of an older puppy or an adult West Highland White Terrier.

Occasionally, breeders will make an older puppy or an adult dog available. That promising show puppy who does not grow up quite as expected may be sold by nine

A shy or noise sensitive puppy can often be found "sitting on the sidelines," watching the action but not participating.

months of age. Keep in mind that he will already have been crate trained, leashed trained, and have a basic understanding of life. An older puppy can be an ideal choice for many situations.

Champions and breeding stock, once retired from active duty, can make an excellent addition to a family household. Most breeders are extremely careful when selecting and interviewing prospective clients for their adult dogs. After all, breeders want to find the perfect home for their Westie who they have shown and loved for five or six years. Be patient and sincere. It can be a difficult time for the breeder to part with an older dog.

Then why do breeders place older Westies? Because they care and love their highlanders. They want them to enjoy and be enjoyed as the only dog or two in a family household. When breeders accumulate large numbers of Westies, it becomes more difficult to give each one individual attention. Most of their time and energy goes to rearing and training the new litter of pups and young show prospects. The retired show dog will make a wonderful companion as he or she will delight in having your undivided attention and will once again be on center stage in your home.

Rescue Westies

There are many rescue organizations across the country.

You can contact the West Highland White Terrier Club of America secretary for a current listing of Westie rescue persons.

The majority of rescue dogs are intact males ranging in age from one to three years. They are usually in need of housebreaking, crate training and formal obedience training. If you are a patient, caring person and have the time to train a highlander in need, this may be a viable option for you. Most rescue organizations charge a nominal fee to cover their veterinary and housing costs of the dogs.

Occasionally, dogs nine years or older are relinquished to rescue. These are the hardest Westies for the rescue persons to place due in part to no one wanting an old dog. If you already own an adult Westie, you may wish or desire to give an old highlander a second chance.

An adult Westie makes a great pet and may fit your lifestyle better than a puppy. Ch. Dawn's Kop N' A Plea, SE, is a beautiful adult Westie owned by Dawn Martin.

Although their time with you may be short, you will know you did your part in making their last few years pleasant and comfortable. There is nothing quite like sharing your life with an older highlander.

WELCOMING Your New Westie

After all the important decisions have been made, the day finally arrives to bring the puppy home. All necessary items should have been purchased in advance and should be situated in the home waiting for the anticipated homecoming. You should be able to find everything you need for your new Westie at your local pet shop. Among these items are:

1. Crate (approximately 18"x20"x17").
2. Blanket made of imitation lambskin or other suitable machine washable material for the bottom of the crate.

Your Westie needs a place to call his own. The Nylabone® Fold-Away Pet Carrier is ideal.

3. Adjustable collar and leash.
4. Puppy food (of the same type the breeder has been feeding).
5. Stainless steel food dishes (1 quart).
6. Safe chew toys: Nylabones® and Nylabone® Flexibles (I do not recommend rawhides).
7. Grooming equipment: puppy slicker brush, metal comb, nail clipper, styptic powder or pencil, rubber bath mat for safe footing.
8. Baby gates to block off any open stairways where a pup could fall or for limiting freedom to a room or two.
9. Designated outside potty area.
10. Clean up supplies for accidents. There are many new products made for puppies that eliminate urine odors completely.

The ideal time to pick up your puppy is first thing in the

Place a blanket in your Westie's crate to help keep him warm. morning. This will allow you a full day to get acquainted. Take along your collar, leash, crate and blanket. Before leaving, be sure the puppy has had a chance to relieve himself then place him in the crate for the ride home. It is unsafe for a puppy to be running loose in a moving car. If he cries at first, don't despair. Most pups settle down quickly and fall asleep when the car is in motion.

The introduction should begin with the immediate family. Do not overwhelm your new puppy the first day. Give him a few days to get to know you and his new house. Then introduce him to outside friends and neighbors over the course of the next few weeks.

Dogs and puppies are creatures of habit. Establish a daily routine with your Westie right from the first day. Make regular potty trips to the designated area often throughout the day. Be sure to lavish praise when he gets it right! It may take a few days of this routine for him to learn his potty area. Be patient. If children are to assume responsibilities for the puppy, it must be with parental supervision.

FEEDING

If possible, continue the feeding schedule already established by the breeder. Any food or feeding changes should be done gradually over the course of a few weeks. Any drastic changes can cause stomach or intestinal upsets resulting in vomiting or diarrhea, both of which are upsetting to you and the puppy and are avoidable.

It is extremely important to feed a high-quality dog food. Occasionally you will encounter a Westie with food allergies. The dog will display a sensitivity in the skin. Symptoms can include reddening of the ears, itchy skin, swollen feet, and/or licking of the feet. Luckily, most Westies respond favorably to an all natural diet consisting of lamb and rice or turkey and barley formula dog foods. Become a label reader. This also applies to treats and dog bones. Next to fleas, the wrong food can be your dog's worst enemy.

CRATE TRAINING

The dog is a den dweller by nature, therefore, he will not soil where he eats or sleeps. A dog, although domesticated by man, still has the instinct for having a den (crate) of his own.

The crate should have a towel or soft blanket (imitation lambskin works well) that can be easily washed and dried. It is important to keep your puppy's environment clean. If you find your pup is having accidents in the crate, chances are the crate is too large. Take a cardboard box and block off the back half of the crate to make it smaller.

The den should be a safe haven where the puppy can relax and play quietly. Safe toys, such as those made by

Nylabones® or Nylabone® Flexibles

High-quality food and plenty of water are essential to a healthy Westie's diet. Feeding changes, if necessary, should be done gradually to avoid any digestive problems.

should be provided in the crate to help with the need for chewing. Care should be taken in the selection of appropriate toys. Some puppies can be destructive and have been known to eat various plastic items, parts of toys, and hunks of rawhide, all of which can have serious consequences. With supervision, squeak toys may be used safely for retrieving games.

Every puppy should have a crate or special area in the house that is his "den." Giving him a place to call his own will make his transition to your home easier.

All young puppies need a lot of sleep. Do not stress and overtire him. During the day he should be periodically placed in the crate to rest. This helps to associate the crate as a den.

It will take several days for your puppy to become accustomed to his new environment and crate. Remember he has just left his mother, littermates, and the only world he has ever known. Patience and perseverance will make the transition easier. You can expect some crying and discontent the first few days. This is normal.

At night it is best to place the puppy in a crate alongside your bed. It has been a long, busy day and the little guy will be tired. Give him a sock stuffed with newspaper to snuggle with. Turn off the lights and say goodnight. Be matter of fact about bedtime, after all it is a part of the daily routine. Should he begin to cry, tap lightly on the crate and say "quiet." Just knowing you are there is reassuring.

The puppy should remain in the crate at night until fully mature. Most Westies are able to handle the transition to a dog bed or your bed by age two years.

HOUSETRAINING

Housebreaking when combined with crate training is an easily accomplished task. A properly housebroken dog is a pleasure to own all the years of his life. Listed below are a few basic rules to follow for quick success:

    1. Rely heavily on your crate for the first week or two.

    2. Limit the area where your puppy can play. One or two

A baby gate can be used to block off doorways and limit the area in which your puppy is allowed to play.

rooms is plenty of space at first.

3. Whenever you take the puppy out of the crate, he should be carried to his special outside area. Don't give your pup the opportunity to get it wrong by having him walk all that distance.

4. Always take the pup to the same potty area. Give the command words such as "hurry-up" or "go potty" repeatedly. This is not the time or the place for play.

5. Praise the puppy when he relieves himself and remove him promptly from the potty area. Within a few short days, the puppy will have caught on and will soon go on command.

6. After going potty, the puppy can be allowed supervised playtime in a specified room or two in the house.

7. For the first few weeks, avoid playing with the puppy outside. Outside is to go potty. Inside is for play. This will help in establishing the house as an extension of his den (crate).

8. Play periods should last no longer than 10-20 minutes without another trip outside. Learn to anticipate his needs so there are no accidents.

9. Should you ever take the puppy to his designated area and he does not go potty, do not bring him in the house and let him run on the floor. If this happens, either hold or crate him for a while then try again. Lavish praise when he gets it right.

10. When an accident happens right before your eyes, give a stern firm "no." Pick up the pup and immediately take him outside. If he finishes while there, praise him. Clean up the accident thoroughly with a product that eliminates all urine odors. If not properly cleaned, a pup will return to the same spot time and time again.

Always take your puppy outside to the same area to relieve himself. He will get used to the designated spot and recognize it as his "potty."

11. If you find a puddle, don't correct your dog after the fact. Just clean it up. A puppy has a very short memory and he will not associate the correction with the accident. All he will know is that you are angry with him. This only leads to confusion. Next time, don't give the pup as much freedom, after all, he must earn that right with good behavior.

12. If you are busy (cooking, cleaning, talking on the phone, etc.) and cannot supervise the pup, he should be placed in his crate.

13. Positive reinforcement is your best tool in housetraining a puppy. Using praise after a job well done works best.

14. Do not keep a young pup crated for more than four hours without a potty break during the day. His bladder and bowel are not fully developed and you will force him to soil his den. If you work, arrangements must be made for a noontime outing.

GROOMING Your Westie

Daily brushing and examining of your Westie has many benefits. It will help to keep his coat sparkling white. He will remain knot and tangle free, making him feel comfortable. Should your Westie's skin become itchy, it will put you on the alert to look for fleas or any skin rashes. Most skin problems, when dealt with properly, can be alleviated quickly. Ignored, they often spell disaster. The act of daily grooming is a pleasure for your dog. When performed as a regular routine, he will delight in his special time spent with you.

THE DAILY ROUTINE

Work Surface

Begin the brushing routine the day you bring him home. Your grooming

A grooming table provides a good surface on which to groom your Westie. A slicker brush and wide tooth metal comb are necessary, as well as scissors in case he needs a trim.

After grooming, your highlander should have the typical Westie expression—dark deep-set eyes peering out from the round "chrysanthemum" face.

surface should be at a comfortable height up off the ground. This will be easier on your back and you will have the advantage over your Westie. After all, he is intelligent and will be less inclined to try to escape or be bad when elevated off the ground. A commercially made grooming table with an attached grooming arm and loop is ideal. Another option is a rubber bath mat atop a washing machine or other suitable work surface. If you opt not to use a grooming table you will need to restrain your Westie by fastening his collar and a short leash to an eye hook that has been securely attached to the wall. *Never* leave your Westie unattended, not even for a moment.

Start by making him stand quietly. Look at his eyes to see that they are bright and clear. Examine the insides of both ears. Any signs of a dark brown discharge should be taken seriously.

The Teeth

Check his teeth by first lifting his lips. Then proceed to opening his mouth wide. Puppies start to lose their baby teeth between 14 and 16 weeks of age. The teething process lasts from four to five months. Having his teeth and mouth handled at a young age will make it easy to clean his second set of teeth later.

Actual cleaning of the teeth should begin at six months of age. There are many products on the market today to make the job easy. A finger brush dipped in peroxide and baking soda works well or a small soft toothbrush. Never use human toothpaste. When swallowed, this can give your dog an upset stomach. There are specially made doggie toothpastes including liver or cheese flavors. Daily brushing of your Westie's teeth will help to avoid costly veterinary cleaning down the road.

Preventive dental care, including regularly brushing and inspecting your Westie's teeth and gums, is the best way to maintain his good oral health.

Nail Trimming

Lift your Westie's feet one by one and examine his nails, between his toes and pads. Toenails should be trimmed once a week. I recommend the use of a safety nail trimmer. This clipper has two cutting surfaces and offers excellent control over how much nail is removed. Guillotine type clippers have only one cutting surface, therefore, they pinch the nail before cutting. Trim just the tips. Cutting too much will make the nail bleed. Should this happen, use styptic powder for prompt results.

Brushing

For brushing I recommend a good quality slicker brush and

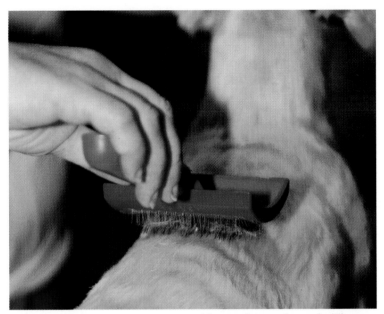

Begin brushing your Westie from behind his head straight down his neck and back to his tail. This motion, repeated three or four times, will stimulate his skin.

wide tooth metal comb. There are many styles to choose from, including designer colors.

Have your Westie stand facing you as you begin brushing him from behind his head straight down his neck to the tail. Repeat the motion three or four times to stimulate his skin. Do the same on both his sides. Then lift one front leg straight forward toward his chin and brush his under carriage.

Be sure to thoroughly brush and comb his arm pits. This area tangles quickly and needs constant attention. While holding his foot, brush the hair on his front legs starting at the top and gradually work down to his foot. Follow brushing with the wide-tooth metal comb. Comb from the foot up making sure all tangles are removed. Repeat on the other side.

Turn your Westie around so he is facing away from you. Brush down his thighs three or four times on each side.

Never pull the rear legs out to the sides. This can create tension on the ligaments that hold the knee cap in place and serious injury could result. Instead, lift one rear leg straight back and brush the under carriage and stomach hair forward.

Continue by brushing the leg hair forward and up in sections all the way down to the foot. Follow by combing from the foot up the leg to the stomach. Repeat on the other side.

On males, pay attention to the hair in front of the penis. If the fur becomes dirty, rub in a little corn starch and then brush thoroughly.

Now your Westie should look all puffed up. Make sure he is standing facing away from you as you comb the side and back leg hair down into place. Once again, have him stand and turn and face you. Comb the front legs down into neat columns.

Now for the head. Hold him under his chin and brush all his facial hair straight back. Repeat three or four times. Then brush forward from the eyes back to the ears. Turn his head to the side and brush up from the eyes down to his neck. Repeat on the other side. After his head is thoroughly brushed out, comb all the head hair straight up. This will give you the typical Westie round chrysanthemum face with deep-set dark eyes peering out at you.

Put him down onto the floor and tell him how wonderful and smart he is. Ask him if he wants to go out and play. His tail will tell you yes!

DRY BATHING

A thorough daily brushing will help in keeping your Westie clean. Should his feet become wet or dirty between professional grooming appointments, he can be dry cleaned. This is a simple task that gives good results.

You will need a towel and a container of corn starch or baby powder. Some baby powders are made with corn starch so read the labels to find the right one.

Put him up on your grooming table or grooming area. Be sure to have a rubber mat under him so he

When brushing your Westie's front legs, lift the leg straight forward and hold onto the foot. Brush up, starting at the top of the leg and working down toward the foot.

Hold your Westie under his chin when brushing his head. Start by brushing the facial hair straight back, brushing each section three or four times.

does not slip. Rub his legs and feet briskly with a towel to absorb as much moisture and dirt as possible.

Brush and comb the leg hair up, then sprinkle the corn starch or baby powder into the fur. Use as much as needed to cover the hair all the way down to the skin. Carry him to his crate and allow him to dry. Do not let him run around the house or you will have corn starch everywhere.

After half an hour or so he will be dry. Put him back up on the grooming area and thoroughly brush out all the corn starch with a slicker or a pin brush. You will be amazed how clean he will be.

The remnants of dirt and corn starch can be easily washed off the rubber mat so it is clean for your next grooming session. With as little as 15 minutes spent, you now have a clean white Westie and have avoided the arduous task of a full bath.

BATHING

Frequent bathing of a Westie with healthy skin is not

recommended. Should the need arise for a full bath in between professional grooming, there are several things to consider. Never use dishwashing liquid or human soap and shampoos. These products are too harsh and are the wrong pH for a dog's skin. Always purchase a high quality shampoo made specifically for dogs. If it is flea season in your area, there are several mild flea shampoos available. Those containing the all natural ingredients found in orange peels readily kill fleas and are safe for both puppies and adult dogs.

Have everything you need ready and close at hand before going to get your Westie. Never call him to come to the tub as he will soon learn not to come at all. Coming to you should always be a pleasurable experience. You will need a rubber bath mat in the bottom of the tub so he does not slip and hurt himself, shampoo for washing, towels for drying and a hose attachment for your tub.

Your Westie should be knot free before being placed in the tub. Small knots quickly become large mats during the bathing process.

Begin by wetting him from the neck down.

Rinsing the Westie's face should always be saved for last—you can see why!

This will give him time to adjust to the water before you start on his head. Put a small amount of shampoo in your hands and rub it gently into his coat.

Start at the back of the neck and work down the body then into his legs. For best results, rub and massage the shampoo all the way through the hair. This massaging action lifts the dirt from the skin and also feels relaxing to your Westie. Continue adding small amounts of shampoo to your hands as you continue along his body and legs. Use enough shampoo to produce a rich lather.

As you wet his head, be careful not to get the water inside his ears. If necessary, fold his ears over and hold them down while wetting or rinsing his head. Once again put a small amount of shampoo in your hands and then apply it to the head and ears. Rub and massage in until you have a rich lather. Never squirt the shampoo

Start bathing your Westie by wetting him from the neck down and massaging the shampoo into a lather that will penetrate his coat and remove the dirt from his skin.

directly onto the head. If the dog moves, you could end up squirting shampoo into his eyes. This can cause an ulceration to the cornea. Always put the shampoo on your hand and then massage it into the head.

Now it's time for the rinsing. Do not have your dog stand in a tub of water and scoop dirty soapy water over him. Start at the back of the neck and rinse with a lot of clean water all the way down to the tail. Squeeze out the water and rinse again. Repeat this on the sides, stomach and legs. Be sure to remove all traces of shampoo. Finally, rinse his head, taking care not to get water in his ears. As you do rinse his face, he will probably shake. Now you know why this is saved until last. After he is rinsed completely, squeeze as much water out of the legs, stomach and head furnishings as possible. Wrap your Westie in a big towel and carry him to your regular grooming area.

Once you have placed him on the rubber matted area, secure him to the wall with a short leash. The last thing you need is a wet Westie doing the mad dash through the house. Starting with the head and ears, towel him dry with a brisk rubbing motion. Continue down the back, then the legs and stomach. The more moisture you can remove with a towel, the less time you will need to spend with a hair dryer.

BLOW DRYING

How the hair is blown dry will determine how good your Westie looks later. For instance, if you do nothing and allow your Westie to air dry, he will more than likely end up looking stringy with his head flat and split down the middle. The end result is not pretty or typical of a Westie.

Begin by combing through the coat to separate all the hairs. Comb the back down flat. The legs can be combed up or down depending on how many furnishings he has. A dog with a lot of hair should be combed down, while one who lacks hair can be combed up on the legs. This will give a fuller look to the leg hair.

You will need a pin brush and a dryer with a lot of airflow. The volume of air delivered is much more important than a high temperature when drying a dog's hair. A dog's skin is very sensitive. Never use the hottest setting. Doing so will inevitably burn the skin before the hair is completely dry.

Start at the back of his neck and blow the hair down flat. Gently brush the top coat with the pin brush. This separates the hair to the skin and helps to dry it faster. Always brush the top coat straight back toward the tail and down on the sides. The direction that the hair dries is how it will lie later. Once the neck, back, tail, and sides are completely dry, you can

Towel dry your Westie briskly, removing as much moisture as possible. The more you can dry him with a towel, the less time you will have to spend with a blow dryer.

begin work on the stomach and legs.

To dry the stomach, have the dog standing with his side facing you. Reach half way under his stomach and lift the skirt up with one hand while you blow the hair dry on his under carriage. When the center is completely dry, brush another small layer of hair down with the pin brush and then dry as before. Continue brushing then blowing until all of the side furnishings are dry. Do small sections at a time to ensure thorough drying.

Comb through your Westie's coat to separate all of the hairs before blow drying.

Brushing the top coat with a pin brush while blow drying will separate the hairs and help the coat to dry faster.

Blow the hair dry in a downward motion on the tops of the front legs to avoid having it look like his elbows are sticking out. The hip and hair on the back end is brushed and dried down and forward. There is nothing quite so

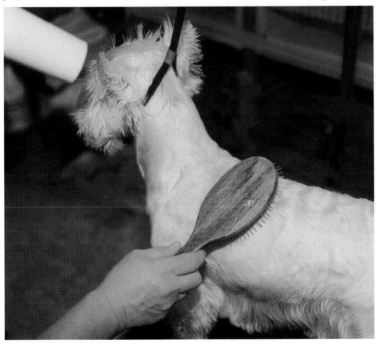

funny looking as a Westie with all his furnishings blown dry straight up. It looks like he is wearing a hula skirt.

After the body, sides, stomach and tops of all the legs are completely dried in a downward direction, you are ready to finish his legs and feet. If he lacks leg hair and you want it to look fuller, brush and blow the hair up on his feet and legs.

Particular attention is needed when blow drying the head to avoid a part or separation. It is important to dry the hair all the way down to the skin. The addition of a small amount of mousse or gel will help the hair to stay standing up.

The Westie's body hair should be brushed and dried downward—a Westie with his hair dried straight up will have a "hula skirt" appearance.

Because you are dealing with gravity, you are in constant battle with trying to make the head furnishings stand up and out. With a Westie whose haircut is long overdue, it will be much more difficult to obtain the desired results than with one who is trimmed every six to eight weeks.

FLEAS, SKIN PROBLEMS, AND MEDICATED BATHS

Fleas

Should fleas or skin rashes occur, they are best dealt with promptly. Do not wait and hope it will go away. They will only become worse in a brief amount of time.

A mild flea shampoo will quickly eradicate fleas from the dog. Start with the head and ears to prevent the fleas from crawling down into the ear canals. Then completely shampoo and lather the body and legs. Let the dog stand with the shampoo on for a full ten minutes. Rinse thoroughly and dry. Next you will need to eliminate the fleas from the environment. The key to success is in breaking the flea life cycle. There are many new products on the market that contain not only fast killing ingredients but also slow working insect growth regulators (IGR). These products, when used aggressively, stop fleas in their tracks and continue working by preventing the flea larvae from developing into adult biting fleas. All indoor areas must be treated including rugs, furniture, bedding, his crate, your car, etc.

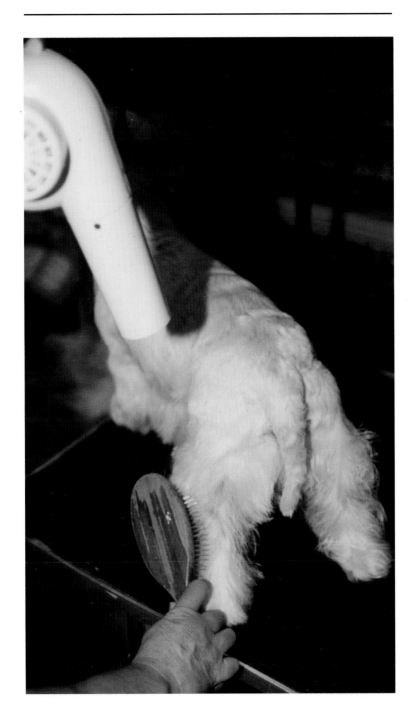

Outdoor lawn products containing beneficial nematodes are not poisonous to the environment. These microscopic nematodes feed on the flea larvae and can survive up to one month in your yard.

If the product you choose to use does not contain an IGR, chances are you will need to repeat the application several times in two week intervals. Fleas are very persistent and can be difficult to eliminate without your perseverance.

Flea Bite Dermatitis

Many breeds of dogs are allergic to flea bites. When a flea bites a dog, it actually slits the skin with the razor sharp edge of its mouth. The flea's saliva contains an anticoagulant, which keeps the slit area bleeding. This allows the flea to feed on the dog's blood. A dog who is sensitive to

Before treatment, Lucky was crawling with fleas, had lost most of her hair, and had swollen, infected skin.

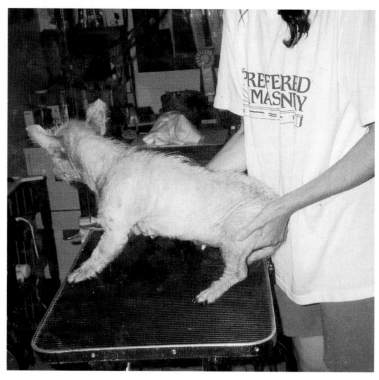

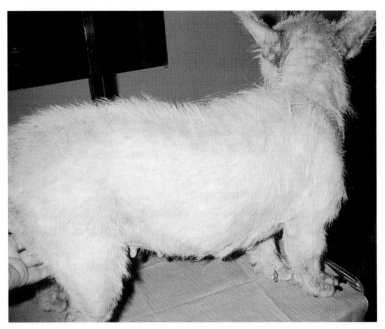

Two weeks after beginning a regime of antibiotics, medicated baths, and an all-natural diet, Lucky's skin showed some healing and her hair had started to grow back.

flea saliva will become itchy shortly after being bitten. Add a few more fleas and you will have a dog who chews, bites, and scratches madly. If the situation is not dealt with promptly, this can and will lead to flea bite dermatitis.

Day One A West Highland White Terrier was relinquished to Westie rescue in August of 1993. She was scheduled to be put down due to "incurable Westie allergies." Since she was crawling with fleas, she was scrubbed and bathed. Her skin was infected, swollen, and hot to the touch. She had little or no hair on most of her body.

Lucky, as she was later named, was put on a diet of all natural lamb and rice dog food. The veterinarian put her on a four week regime of an antibiotic. She was bathed daily by alternating benzoyl peroxide shampoo one day and a medicated sulfur/salicylic acid shampoo the next. In addition to bathing, her swollen feet and ears were dabbed with betadine solution.

Two Weeks In just two weeks time, Lucky's body skin was beginning to heal. Her lower legs, feet and ears still showed evidence of swelling, so the daily bathing and betadine treatments continued in these areas. Overall bathing of her body was reduced to twice a week.

Four Weeks By four weeks, new hair had begun to grow and Lucky was given a new lease on life. General bathing with the medicated sulfur/salicylic acid shampoo was reduced to once a week. The feet continued to have daily bathing and betadine treatments.

One and a half years after her bout with flea bite dermatitis, Lucky is fully covered with hair and her skin shows normal pigmentation. This Westie lived up to her name!

Six Weeks after her rescue, Lucky was placed with an understanding couple where she remains today. She continues eating an all natural diet of lamb and rice dog food. In spite of occasionally licking her feet and being sensitive to flea bites, she is happy, healthy and enjoys living life to the fullest.

One and a Half Years Finally, one and a half years later, Lucky was fully covered with hair and displaying normal dark pigmented skin on her ears, pads, and stomach.

Skin Rashes

Small skin rashes, when dealt with promptly, are often cleared in three or less treatments. The course of action you choose is dependent on the type of rash present. Treatments most commonly consist of a combination of cleaning the area daily with a medicated shampoo or solution then applying a topical ointment or a drying medicated powder. Any time there is a breakdown in the skin, it is most

Four weeks after beginning treatment, Lucky's hair growth and skin condition showed improvement and the frequency of her medicated baths was reduced to once a week.

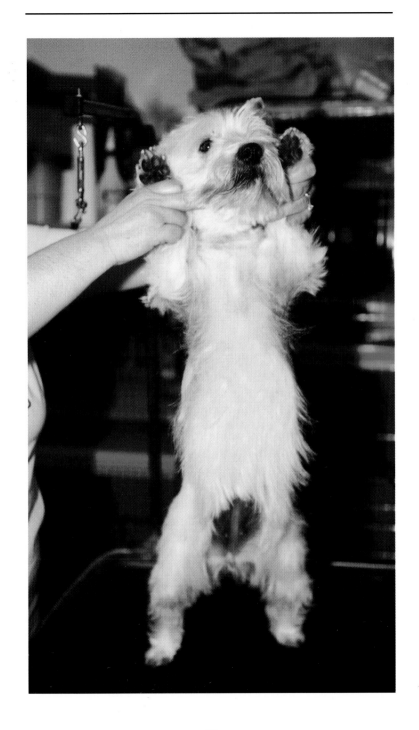

important to keep the area spotlessly clean. This aids in the healing process and you can often avoid a secondary bacterial skin infection.

Never delay veterinary care for major problems or in the event your small skin rash fails to respond and start healing after one or two days. Avoid using over-the-counter shampoo solutions or ointments containing steroids. Cortisone, a common steroid, may stop the itch fast, but its use will interfere with the dog's natural healing ability and immune system. Healing can be delayed or sometimes halted completely. Steroids should be used only with the advisement of your veterinarian.

Always buy high-quality dog shampoos, not shampoos intended for human use. There are many types of medicated shampoos available. Each has a specific purpose so read the labels.

Oatmeal shampoos relieve itchy dry skin and are very soothing. They are gentle and can safely be used frequently on all skin types.

Tar (sometimes contains sulfur) is a deep penetrating antiseborrheic shampoo that works well for itchy, oily skin. It is quite harsh, therefore, it should only be used on dogs with greasy, oily skin at approximately one week intervals.

Medicated shampoos containing the combination of sulfur and salicylic acid are used for daily cleansing of chronic or severe skin problems. These have a debriding action that aids in the removal of dead layers of skin. Continued daily use will lead to the exposure of healthy new skin. Chronic and severe problems can take several weeks of this regime to clear. Beware of the pitfalls of stopping treatment too soon.

Benzoyl peroxide shampoo is often recommended and prescribed by veterinarians when secondary skin infections are present. Common signs include pus oozing from the pores. The skin itself is often swollen, has hair loss, and may be thick like leather. There is usually a distinctive pungent odor indicative of infection. Oral antibiotic therapy is a must for this condition to improve. Consult your veterinarian.

Iodine shampoo is an excellent choice for cleansing scrapes, cuts and minor open wounds. It aids in killing fungus and bacteria on the skin surface.

For overall itchy skin, best results are obtained by bathing the entire body. All medicated shampoos need to be soaked on the skin for a prescribed amount of time in order to be effective. Read and follow label directions.

When daily bathing of chronic or severe problems becomes necessary, you need only bathe those areas that are affected. Healthy/normal skin should not be bathed repeatedly with any of the above listed medicated shampoos, with the exception of the oatmeal shampoo.

Betadine 10% solution or povidine is available without prescription at most drug stores. These products are effective against most bacteria, viruses, fungi and yeast. When applied full strength, it has a drying effect. For chronic or severe conditions, it works best when dabbed on with a cotton ball right after being dried from the daily bath. The iodine products will stain synthetic materials so be sure to dry it completely before releasing your dog for a romp in the house.

Always use a shampoo that is specially formulated for dogs. There are many shampoos available; your veterinarian can advise you which one to use.

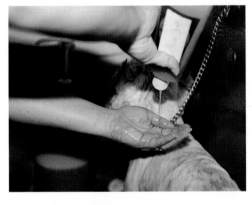

Foot Licking

Foot licking in Westies can quickly become an annoying habit. It is often the first sign of a problem. The dog licks his feet because they itch. The wet from his tongue temporarily relieves the itch. The wet warm feet are ideal habitat for fungi and yeast infections, similar to athlete's foot. Fungi and yeast infections itch and so the cycle continues.

To stop the itch, make a solution of one part betadine or povidine and four parts water. Soak the feet daily for 10 to 15 minutes. Treatment must continue for several weeks. The longer the dog has been licking and biting his feet, the longer your treatments will need to continue. After soaking his feet, rinse them with warm water, towel dry, then blow dry. If his feet become wet from outside during the day, dry them off every time he comes in. Do not encourage or allow an environment for fungi and yeast to live and thrive.

PROFESSIONAL GROOMERS

Groomers and grooming shops come in a variety of shapes and sizes. It is important to select one that suits your personal requirements. Call and make arrangements to visit groomers in your area. They are listed under pet grooming in the Yellow Pages. Explain that you would like to take 10 minutes of their time to stop by and talk. If you cannot keep the appointment, be considerate and call to cancel.

All shops should offer neat surroundings both inside and outside. There should be little or no offensive odors. Holding cages are available that are secure and easy to clean. Overhead fluorescent lighting is a big plus. The groomer should be a caring individual with whom you can communicate freely. After all, your Westie will be visiting this person every six to eight weeks for many years to come.

If your dog is clipped by the same person on a regular basis he will become relaxed and comfortable while at the grooming shop. He knows what is expected and that you will return for him. The groomer will in turn become familiar with him and might be your first line of defense should any changes occur in him. They can alert you to fleas, weight loss, or other health issues. A groomer's life is surrounded by dogs and they are a wealth of knowledge.

Grooming shops will often have holding cages for dogs. These two Westies are patiently awaiting their owners' return.

Westies as a breed are not as common as Poodles, Cocker Spaniels, or Miniature Schnauzers in the grooming shop. Do not be dismayed if your highlander comes home looking like another breed. Rest assured his coat will grow back quickly and you can try again. Remember you selected this groomer because you felt good about him and you could communicate freely. So now is the time to speak up. Take this book with you. It offers many examples of well groomed Westies throughout its pages. Then kick back and be patient. The art of Westie grooming takes time to perfect. If after three or four regular groomings at six to eight week intervals, you find the professional you selected is unable or unwilling to fine-tune his skills, choose a new groomer.

If you plan to show your Westie, you must have his coat hand plucked. You may have trouble locating a groomer who does this—look for a terrier specialist.

Occasionally, knowledgeable Westie breeders will offer grooming as a service. If you are lucky enough to locate a breeder/groomer in your area, he is worth his weight in gold.

SHOW GROOMING

Young West Highland White Terriers who are destined for the conformation show ring must have their coats hand plucked. Hand plucking retains the natural harsh texture of the coat. The hair needs to be worked a minimum of once every two weeks to keep the coat rolling. It is an extremely time consuming endeavor and is quickly becoming a dying art. Very few professional groomers have the time or the inclination to do hand plucking. Should you wish to have your West Highland White Terrier hand plucked, you will need to find a terrier specialist.

Ask your breeder for names of terrier handlers in your area or attend several dog shows. Watch all the terrier breeds while they are being judged. Then speak with as many terrier handlers as possible. Be considerate and wait patiently until they have a spare moment to speak with you. Dog shows can be hectic for a busy handler.

BASIC TRAINING for Your Westie

Training a Westie good manners is not only challenging but is a very rewarding endeavor as well. With his heritage of hunting wild game deep in the rocks and caverns of the earth, he is very into self-preservation and independent thinking. You need to understand his independent nature and to be flexible in your selection of training methods.

To begin, you will need to have his undivided attention. This is number one of the two keys to canine learning. Keep your training sessions brief: 5 to 10 minutes two or three times daily.

When first teaching a new exercise or command, do so in an area free of outside distraction. There will be plenty of time later, after he has learned his new skills, to show off for your friends and neighbors.

Training your Westie is a necessity. A few brief training sessions each day will teach your Westie good manners and give you and your dog time to get to know each other.

MOTIVATION

The second key to training your Westie is motivation. This you must provide for all your training sessions. Motivation comes in many forms and you will need to find which combinations work best for your dog's personality. Remember his independent nature and through proper motivation you can make training and learning *his* idea. Keep your session fun, interesting, positive and upbeat. Never train when you are in a bad mood or angry. He will know.

You might ask yourself, "What will motivate my highlander to higher degrees of learning?" I have had success with several of the following suggestions. Bear in mind each dog is an individual, and what works for one may not work for another. Be innovative and experiment. After all, who knows your Westie better than you?

Food

Food is an excellent choice of motivation for training young puppies. I recommend using their regular dry kibble so you do not upset their digestive system. Start your training sessions just before each regularly scheduled meal. Measure out your Westie's normal portion and use this for training. Any leftovers are to be fed immediately following his learning session. In doing it this way, you will not interrupt his housebreaking routine.

Start your first few lessons inside the house in a familiar area with no distractions. No TV, extra people, or toys lying around.

Put the pup on the floor and wait until he looks up at you. Do not speak, just give him one piece of kibble. As he is eating, you walk away quietly then turn and face him. When he looks up gently call his name, "Puppy come."

Bend your knees and crouch down to his level as he trots over to you. Never lean or loom over the top of your puppy. This is very threatening to him and will teach him not to come too close. When he is directly in front of your legs, praise and release with an "Okay," then give him one piece of kibble. Repeat this no more than four times in a row. Westies quickly become bored with repetition.

To teach the sit, wait until he looks up. Say "sit," as you suspend a piece of kibble one or two inches directly above his head. As he looks up his butt will go down. Praise and release with an "Okay" as you give him the treat. Repeat no more than four times.

End your training session on a positive note and put the pup in his crate to eat the remainder of his meal. The first few lessons should last no longer than one or two minutes and should be done before each feeding.

Food is an excellent puppy motivator. A piece of kibble is often used to teach the sit and other basic commands.

Don't disrupt your Westie's feeding routine by giving him extra food during training. Use the same kibble that he eats at mealtime and take the "treats" from his normal portion.

Food, when used as a motivator, should be kept out of view until a command is given. Never try to bribe the puppy. "Oh please come and sit and I'll give you a treat," Wrong!

Attention first. Then when he is looking at you give the command and place the motivator in the proper position. When the pup gets it right, praise, release with an "Okay," and then give the treat.

Be consistent. Don't overtrain or bore your Westie and soon he will be looking forward to learning as a new adventure in life.

Verbal Praise

Verbal praise can be used by itself or in combination with other motivators. Verbal praise should be given with enthusiasm and sincerity. It is the one motivator you will always have wherever the two of you go.

Body language includes how you stand, walk, stop, bend,

etc. Dogs as a species communicate with each other primarily with body language. They know and learn to understand our moods through observations and experience.

It bears additional mention—never train your dog when you are angry. He will know. When you train with confidence and fairness, your Westie will respond with happiness and confidence.

Bird Feathers

A bird feather can be an excellent motivator when you start to heel with your Westie puppy. I recommend heeling training to begin after one or two weeks of teaching the sit and come. By this time your highlander will be looking forward to learning something new.

At first, the puppy may have a tendency to jump at the feather—this is fine as long as you have his attention.

Begin in a distraction free area so your Westie has every opportunity to get it right. Do one or two sits and recalls to get his attention focused on you.

Position yourself so the dog is by your left side, give the command "puppy heel." As you step out, dangle the feather in your right hand slightly forward and out from the left knee. Walk straight forward two or three steps at first, praise and release.

It is normal for puppies to jump and leap forward at the feather. This is fine, after all, the object is to move ahead while holding his attention.

For several weeks, walk in a straight line only. Gradually increase your distance each day while keeping his attention focused on you. Corners and turns can be taught at a later time. In just a few short weeks your highlander will be ready to learn and perform in places away from home and around other dogs and people.

A bird feather will keep your Westie's attention when teaching the heel. With the pup on your left side, dangle the feather in front of him and start by walking a few steps at a time.

OBEDIENCE CLASSES

Being the fun loving clown that

he is, you will find that a well-mannered Westie is an added delight to most family outings. His level of training will be reflected in his everyday behavior at home and away. So let's discuss formal obedience classes.

Obedience schools and classes are available in most areas. They are offered as a community service by many nonprofit dog clubs, SPCAs, and YMCAs and can be found in the classified section of the newspaper under "*pet handling.*" Boarding kennels with private trainers will be listed in the Yellow Pages of your phone book.

KINDERGARTEN PUPPY TRAINING

This is geared for puppies of all breeds between the ages of eight weeks and four months. The classes offer socialization with a variety of different breeds and sizes of puppies in a controlled setting. Here your Westie pup will learn the basic commands.

The recall, or "come," is one of the most important commands you will teach your Westie. When your puppy comes to you, give him lots of praise—he deserves it!

Heel

Remember your motivators and keep your Westie's attention on you. It will be challenging but the reward of him looking up at you will be worth every bit. You, in turn, must pay attention to him at all times while in the class. Do not let your mind run astray or your highlander will be sure to take advantage of your slip-up. During heeling exercises, your pup will learn right, left, and about turns and to sit at your side when you stop.

Come

This is a fun recall where the instructor restrains the puppy by his collar while you leave him and walk across the room. Once at the other side of the room you crouch down real low

The stand is taught with you kneeling by your Westie's side. Once again, a piece of kibble is used for motivation.

at puppy eye level and excitedly call him. When the puppy starts struggling and wiggling to get to you, the instructor will let go of his collar. Your young highlander will come bounding toward you. Let him jump on you and encourage him to do so by petting and stroking his sides as he puts his front paws on you. "Aren't you the most wonderful dog to have come all that distance. What a good boy!" Your Westie should think he has found the pot of gold at the end of the rainbow.

Remember, the recall or come command is one of the most important exercises you can teach your Westie. It could save his life.

Sit, Down, and Stand Stay

All are done as group exercises. Your Westie will be taught to sit, lie down, and stand in a line with all the other puppies. During the sit and down he will have to hold his position while you leave him and stand out in front of him. Be sure he holds his position when you return to him, then release him with an

The fun retrieve is an enjoyable game and good confidence builder for your Westie. After your puppy picks up the toy, call him to come to you and reward him with praise.

"okay." The stand is taught with you kneeling by his side. He must learn to accept a stranger approaching and touching his head and back.

Fun Retrieve

The fun retrieve is just that — all fun and games. You will need a toy or ball of a size which your Westie pup can pick up and carry with ease. Get his attention focused on the toy by shaking or dragging the toy in front of him. When he starts grabbing at the toy, toss it out about 4 feet. As he picks up the toy, call him to you with quiet praise and enthusiasm. Your Westie should be on leash so you can gently reel him in should he choose not to give up his treasure. Remember, you make the rules by which to play.

Occasionally, you will find a Westie pup who refuses to pick up the toy you have chosen. After exhausting all possible objects (leather, fur squeak toy, sock, etc.) buy your Westie a German-Shepherd-size plain old- fashioned dog biscuit. Work your puppy on retrieving before mealtime. Give him time to sniff and gnaw on the treat. When he is ready to settle in and chew away, take hold of one end of the biscuit and slowly wiggle it away and then slide it about 2 feet in front of him. Do not speak as you do this. When he trots out to the bone, stay very still and quiet. Do not distract him in any way. When the bone is in his mouth, softly call him to you with gentle praise. Most Westie pups who do not retrieve lack confidence. Gentle praise and encouragement works wonders for building your Westie's self esteem.

Socialization

Interacting with puppies of different breeds in a controlled setting is a wonderful experience for your young West Highland White Terrier. He will learn social manners and be more accepting of other dogs when he matures.

Supervised socialization is a part of many puppy classes. Your Westie will mingle with all kinds of puppies, and as a result, be more well-adjusted to other dogs as he grows up.

During classroom socialization, the owners will often sit or kneel in a large circle. The puppies are placed in the center and are allowed to mingle with each other. This is always supervised by all owners and the instructor. No bullying or aggressive behavior is to be tolerated.

Shy or less outgoing pups are held briefly and then passed from their owner to the person on the right. This person, in turn, pets the youngster and talks in a soft pleasant tone of voice, then passes the pup to the next and so on around the circle. Most pups love attention and soon realize there is nothing to fear. Within a week or two, they will be ready to join in the fun of the play circle.

Most Kindergarten Puppy Training classes are a half an hour in duration. They meet once a week for six to eight weeks.

What a puppy learns at a young age will be remembered the rest of his life. Kindergarten Puppy Training is one of the most important classes for learning good social behavior.

SUB-NOVICE OR BEGINNER CLASS

This first level obedience class is for all breeds of dogs six months of age and older. Classes are one hour long and meet once a week for six to eight weeks. Although Kindergarten Puppy Training is not required, your Westie will be ahead of the game with the training you have already done at home.

All training is done on a 6 foot long obedience leash, and your Westie should wear a rolled leather buckle collar or a choke chain. A choke chain is a training collar and should be used as such. Never leave your Westie unattended while wearing this collar. Not even in his crate.

Heeling

Your Westie will learn to walk on a loose lead at your left side. He will be taught to sit squarely by your left leg when you stop. You, in turn, will learn the finer points of foot work. These

The down/stay is taught as a group exercise with the dogs lined up next to each other.

In the down/stay, the dog stays down as the handler walks around him and returns to the heel position. include the left turn, right turn, and about turn, and which foot to stop and start forward on. The foot you use when heeling forward with your highlander should be the opposite of the one you use when he is left on a stay command.

How will my Westie know the difference between the left and right foot? Body language, that's how dogs communicate through and understand the subtle changes in how we move. If you are consistent with your feet while training, your Westie will learn to anticipate your every move.

The slow pace teaches the dog to stay by your side while moving slowly. This is very useful when walking in a crowded area. The fast pace is just that – breaking stride and trotting forward. It sure comes in handy when you are in a hurry.

Sit and Down Stays

The stays are taught as a group exercise with the dogs lined up 3 to 4 feet apart. They will learn to sit for a full minute and stay down for three minutes with the handler at the end of a 6 foot leash. Your Westie must hold his position as you walk by and around him back into heel position. Always release him with an "okay" when the exercise is over.

Stand/Stay

In this exercise, your Westie is taught to stand for examination while you go to the end of your 6 foot training lead. He must stay in the stand position while a stranger touches his head, shoulders, and rump. Your Westie must hold his position as you walk by and around him back into heel position.

Formal Come Command

You will leave your Westie on a sit/stay, go to the end of the leash, face him, then call his name, "Westie come." He will be taught to come and sit directly in front of you.

Finish

The finish command teaches the dog to move from in front of you back into the heel position.

In the stand/stay, the dog is taught to stand for examination and remain standing until the handler returns to the heel position.

NOVICE CLASS

This is a second level obedience class. The classes are usually one hour long and meet once a week for six to eight weeks. What you learn in this session are all of the necessary requirements your Westie would need to compete in the Novice Class of obedience for his Companion Dog title.

Heeling on the leash is a Novice Class exercise that includes executing turns and changing pace. When you stop, your Westie should sit by your left side.

If this is the first dog you are training, you will most likely need to repeat this class two or three times before you and your highlander are ready to enter an obedience trial. All West Highland White Terriers with AKC full or limited registration are eligible to compete at American Kennel Club obedience trials. Neutered dogs are allowed and are encouraged to participate. So, what will you learn and what is needed to show your highlander in the novice class at an obedience trial?

Heel on Leash and Figure Eight

This is a heeling pattern combining all of the elements you learned in your first class. You and your highlander will heel at a normal pace while executing the right, left, and about turns. The pattern will include two changes of pace. The slow and the fast, where your Westie must keep up or slow down to maintain a loose lead between you. When you stop, the dog is to sit squarely by your left side.

The figure eight will be taught in this session. It involves having two people stand 8 feet apart. The dog and you walk at a normal pace around each person and cross over in the middle forming a figure eight. This pattern is done twice with at least one stop in the center.

Stand for Examination

The stand that you had learned before will now be done off leash. You will stand your Westie, tell him to stay, walk out 6 feet, turn, and face him. He will be required to hold his position while the judge touches his head, shoulders and rump. He must continue to stand as you walk past and around him back into heel position.

Heel Off Leash

This requires the same elements as the heel on leash including pace changes and turns. The figure eight is not included in this exercise.

Recall

Your Westie will be placed on a sit/stay as you walk 30 to 40 feet away. After you turn and face him, the judge will signal you to call your dog. Your highlander must come readily at a brisk pace and sit in front of your legs. On order of the judge you will finish your dog. He must move smartly from in front back into heel position.

Sit/Stay

This is done as a group exercise with up to 12 dogs lined up at one end of the ring. The handlers are required to sit their dogs and leave their dogs as a group. You will walk across the ring, turn and face your dog. The dogs are required to sit and stay for one full minute and must hold their sit while the handlers return around the dogs' backs into heel position.

Long Down/Stay

The dogs are sitting in a line with up to 12 dogs in the ring. When instructed by the judge, the handlers will down their dogs as a group. You will then leave your highlander and walk across the ring and turn to face your Westie. He must remain in the down position for a full three minutes, then hold his down

In the Novice Class, the sit/stay is more advanced. The dogs are lined up and must remain sitting while the handlers walk across the room, wait for one minute, and return to heel.

while the handlers return to their dogs.

Whether or not you decide to compete with your Westie for his Companion Dog title, training your highlander at this level can be a wonderful rewarding experience. Just think, in but a few short months of training, you will have a West Highland White Terrier of which you can proudly take anywhere. The rewards of early training will last throughout his entire lifetime.

Add a few tricks to his repertoire of learning and your highlander will be ready to entertain both friends and family.

Some dogs will invent their own tricks—this Westie fetches his leash and brings it to his owner when he's ready to go for a walk.

TRICKS

I have yet to meet a Westie who did not delight in performing a trick or two. Tricks can be as simple as retrieving a tennis ball or as complex as you can dream of. You are only limited by your own imagination and the West Highland White Terrier's short legs.

I have included a few suggestions for you to try.

Sitting Pretty

This involves teaching the dog to sit up and beg. It is best taught with a tempting morsel of food. Have your Westie sit while you suspend the food above his head. Instruct him to get it as you lower then raise the morsel as he reaches for it. In no time at all he will be sitting pretty.

Jump Through a Hoop or Your Arms

This is best taught by placing a hoop in a doorway, thus preventing your Westie from going around instead of through the hoop. Start with the hoop sitting on the floor. Call your highlander to you and tell him "jump" as he crosses through the hoop. Give lots of praise and encouragement when he gets it right. Keep the hoop low and in the doorway for several weeks till you are sure he understands the command "jump."

Gradually raise the hoop several inches until your Westie is jumping with glee.

Now it is time to remove the hoop from the doorway. Start with it low and gradually increase the height. Never raise the hoop or your arms so high that your Westie might hurt himself.

Keep it fun and use lots of praise, better yet have your friends and family clap their approval. West Highland White Terriers are very proud and they do love applause.

Your Westie will be proud to perform his repertoire of tricks for your family and friends as long as he gets lots of praise and applause. A treat is also a great reward.

Shoot the Dog or Play Dead

Once your Westie has learned the down command, you are only one step away from teaching this trick.

Start with your arm raised. Slowly lower your arm and take aim with your finger as you give the down command. Walk up to your Westie and as you give the command "bang," gently push him onto his side with your gun finger. Tell him stay. Sympathize with the dead dog, "Oh! The poor thing, what a shame, etc." Then release him with an "okay" as he springs back to life. Repeat three or four times everyday until he understands.

Soon you will be able to drop the "down" and "stay" commands. The end result is a Westie who drops to his side as you shoot him with a "bang" and remains there till released. This trick is a real crowd pleaser and is quite easy to teach.

Other Suggestions

Roll over or shake hands are common Westie tricks. I even know a Westie who fetches his leash when he wants to go for a walk. Be fair, teach one trick at a time. Do not confuse him with learning multiple tricks at the same time.

Ch. Dawn's Manhattan Project, JE, is a pro at "sitting pretty."

ACTIVITIES for the Westie

If you enjoy being outside and taking long walks, there are many enjoyable activities for you and your dog. A weekend away with your favorite white terrier, what could be more fun? Many trails and parks do allow dogs, but be sure to phone ahead to confirm their acceptance. Pack a long line or a retractable leash as no dogs, not even your well-behaved highlander, should be running free. Teach him right from the start to stay on the trail and discourage all attempts to wander into the woods.

Westies have been quite successful at tracking. Kent's Little Sass n Back, TD, "Sassie," negotiates a perfect right turn. Owned by Rita M. Kline.

Take drinking water, food and a comb for your Westie. He will need water periodically while on the trail. Carry small plastic bags containing individual pre-measured servings of his food. When empty, the plastic bag can be used for clean up. A comb takes up little space and can come in handy for removing burdock, dirt, etc. from his coat. Most important of all, be considerate and clean up after your dog. Now hit the trails and have fun.

TRACKING

This is an American Kennel Club event. There are three available titles in this area. They are tracking dog/TD, tracking dog excellent/TDX and variable surface tracking/VST. Tracking is a non-competitive sport. In that I mean, all dogs who are entered have an equal chance of earning their title. There are no numerical scores, simply a pass or fail grading system.

Sassie is able to locate the article, a glove, at the end of the track.

The dog's keen sense of smell and ability to follow a human scent has fascinated man for many years. If you enjoy walking and observing your Westie, this may be a fun adventure for you both.

The basic requirements for a TD title include that the dog must follow an aged scent left by a person who is called a track layer. The track layer begins by leaving a small flag on a pole at the start of the track and another approximately 30 yards along the track to indicate the direction to proceed. Most TD tracks are 440 to 500 yards in length and contain both left and right turns. At the end, the track layer deposits a glove or wallet for the dog to find.

The dog wears a non-restrictive harness that is attached to a long line of 30 to 40 feet in length. The handler is to remain at least 20 feet behind the dog and is not to guide or lead the dog in any manner.

Tracking is one of the few events in which you must trust and rely on the dog for direction. Westies through the years have done exceedingly well in this endeavor.

BOATING

Westies are very adaptable and have little or no problems adjusting to a boating experience. Take along plenty of cool drinking water. Bright sun on the water can make a dog thirsty. Your highlander should wear a buckle collar and lead at all times. He should be taught to sit quietly so as not to end up the "dog overboard." Doggy lifejackets are available in a Westie size and I highly recommend their use. Here's to warm breezes and clear sailing!

AGILITY

Agility is now an approved American Kennel Club event. It is virtually a doggie obstacle course. Obstacles include jumps of varying types, tunnels both open and flat, balance beam, teeter–totter, weave poles, a resting platform, A-frame, etc. It is a fast paced, timed event with both dog and handler needing strength and endurance. Competition of this type requires a Westie with a high energy level who is in excellent physical condition. If you and your highlander enjoy life in the fast lane, this event could be for you.

PLAY BALL

West Highland White Terriers have a distinct fondness for balls of all sizes. A tennis ball can give pleasure, entertainment, and exercise inside the home on bad weather days. Most Westies enjoy a good game of chase and fetch. It should be noted that some have been known to defuzz a tennis ball when ignored.

Versatile Westies adapt well to boating, and many enjoy it. For a safe outing, make sure that your Westie is kept on a lead and that he wears his "doggy" lifejacket.

A big rubber ball in an enclosed fenced area is a wonderful way to exercise and play with a Westie. Kicking the ball once or twice is all that is needed to start the game. This type of ball play should always be supervised so your highlander does not exhaust himself.

Earthdog Trials

The American Kennel Club added earthdog trials to its list of performance events on October 1, 1994. Prior to this date, the American Working Terrier

Ch. Kirkton Connecticut Yankee and Dartagnian's Tartan Lass, CDX, take a break at the end of a tunnel.

Kirkton's Conundrum, NA, SE, owned by Lynn W. Stonesifer and Allison A. Platt, makes it over the A-frame at an agility trial.

Association offered a go to ground title called a certificate of gameness (CG). The CG was equivalent to a junior earthdog title. The purpose of these trials

In a Junior Earthdog test, the dog is released 10 feet from the tunnel, which is 9 inches by 9 inches and 30 feet long.

is to prove our West Highland White Terriers still retain their basic instinct and willingness to go to ground. All tests are conducted using a manmade tunnel in a controlled setting. The dogs are never exposed to the hazards of a natural earth den with live badgers or fox.

The method of scoring for this event is a simple pass/fail. All West Highland White Terriers, Dachshunds, and other eligible terrier breeds have an equal chance of demonstrating their natural hunting instincts and willingness to go to ground.

There are four different classes offered and three available earthdog titles.

Introduction to Quarry

This would be the starting class for a dog who has never seen a tunnel or quarry before. The tunnel is constructed of wood measuring 9 inches high by 9 inches wide by 10 feet long with one right angle turn. At the end of the tunnel behind bars in a protected cage are two adult rats or a properly scented artificial mechanism capable of movement, either of which constitutes the quarry.

The dog is released on the ground 10 feet from the entrance of the den. The dog is allowed two minutes from the time he enters the den to start working the quarry. He must continue working for 30 seconds in order to pass. Work includes any or all of the following: digging, scratching, barking, lunging or biting at the bars in front of the quarry.

Junior Earthdog Test

This tunnel is also 9 inches by 9 inches, but is now 30 feet in length with three turns. There are no previous requirements necessary for entry in this class and a dog may be entered in both this test and in the introduction to quarry at the same trial.

Author Dawn Martin and a happy Junior Earthdog qualifier! To earn the Junior Earthdog title, a dog must receive two passing scores under two different judges.

The dog is released on the ground 10 feet from the den entrance. The dog has 30 seconds to reach the quarry and another 30 seconds to begin working. Once work has commenced, a dog must continue working for a full 60 seconds. A dog who qualifies in all of the above is awarded a passing score. Two passing scores under two different judges are needed to earn the Junior Earthdog title (JE).

Senior Earthdog Test

Once a dog has earned the JE title, he is now eligible to enter the senior class.

This test is more difficult with the addition of a false den and a false exit located at the second and third turn off the main tunnel. The entrance to the tunnel is surrounded by a mound of earth at least 4 inches higher then the top of the tunnel liner. This not only hides the entrance from the dog's view, but provides for a steeper entrance into the den.

The dog is released 20 feet from the entrance and has a total of 90 seconds to find the entrance and reach the quarry. He must work the quarry continuously for 90 seconds. After working the required time the quarry is removed from the liner. The handler has a total of 90 seconds to call his dog out of the tunnel and pick him up.

Any dog who qualifies in all three areas, 90 seconds to quarry, 90

After a dog has his Junior Earthdog title, he is eligible to move on to the senior test. A mound of earth around the tunnel entrance is one example of the advanced difficulty.

This group of Westies had a successful day at an earthdog trial. Owned by Thom and Amy Juzwik, Lynn Stonesifer, Allison Platt, Lou Herczeg, Dawn Martin, and Patti Marks.

seconds working, and 90 seconds to return to handler, shall be awarded a passing score. Three passing scores under at least two different judges are needed to earn the Senior Earthdog title (SE).

Master Earthdog Test

After a dog has completed the requirement for the SE title, he becomes eligible to enter the master level of competition.

This is the hardest level and combines those elements an earthdog would need to hunt in a natural setting.

All dogs are run in pairs. The dogs are released together 100 feet from the den entrance. The handlers and judge proceed forward toward the blocked den entrance. There is an unscented false tunnel along the way that is visible to the dogs. In spite of this, the dogs must find the blocked scented entrance before the judge gets there.

The first dog to indicate the entrance is allowed to run,

while the other is staked 10 feet from the entrance. The staked dog must honor the working dog and should not bark excessively.

In addition to the false den and false exit of the senior test, there are two additional obstacles in the tunnel: a construction point of 18 inches in length where the tunnel narrows to 6 inches and an obstruction. The obstruction is placed across the tunnel in such a way as to move up or down when pushed upon. This allows the dog access with effort to pass the obstruction and continue to the quarry.

After working the quarry, he is removed and then in turn must honor the second dog's run.

Any dog that finds and indicates the scented blocked entrance, reaches the quarry in 90 seconds, works the quarry for 90 seconds and honors another dog's run will

A visit from a friendly Westie is sure to bring a smile to anyone's face!

be awarded a passing score. Four passing scores under at least two different judges are needed to be qualified for the Master Earthdog title (ME).

PET THERAPY

Pet therapy has become quite popular in the last few years. Many nursing homes and elderly daycare centers welcome well behaved pets.

West Highland White Terriers, with their appealing good looks and pleasant easy going personalities, are a great choice for pet therapy. Their compact size makes for easy lifting to be cuddled, held or petted. They are charming and seem to instinctively know to be gentle. Pet therapy with your Westie will surely show you a compassionate side of your dog that you may not have known existed.

The Westie's friendly personality and compact size make him a wonderful therapy dog. Six-week-old Mike helps to brighten a friend's day.

Take a day, be a volunteer. When you see the smiles, you'll be glad you did.

COLLECTIONS and Collectibles

People can and do collect a wide variety of items. A favorite pastime of many Westie owners is to collect and display items bearing the likeness of their favorite breed–the Westie, of course! Searching for Westie memorabilia is a fun and interesting hobby. Through the years, the West Highland White Terrier has been depicted in various forms of art. Today, it's not surprising to see the Westie portrayed on a wide variety of collectibles. From paintings and prints to post cards and figurines, this breed's impish face can currently be found on coffee mugs, birthday/greeting cards, and articles of clothing. Statues ranging from small to life size can be found in gift shops all across the country. Jewelry made of gold and silver adorn many Westie owners. Rings, watches, bracelets, and earrings, to name a few, are made to perfection with Westie silhouettes and full faces.

Collector's plates, calendars...you never know what you will find next to add to your collection of Westie memorabilia.

Once you find your first Westie treasure, you'll be hooked for life. Part of the fun of collecting Westie items is the excitement of discovering new and unique pieces to add to your assortment. Collecting older pieces can be quite challenging, as they are few and far between. Keep an eye open, you never know what you might find next.

Enjoy your morning coffee with a Westie! Coffee mugs are just one of the many items that bear the Westie's likeness.

SPORT of Purebred Dogs

Welcome to the exciting and sometimes frustrating sport of dogs. No doubt you are trying to learn more about dogs or you wouldn't be deep into this book. This section covers the basics that may entice you, further your knowledge and help you to understand the dog world. If you decide to give showing, obedience or any other dog activities a try, then I suggest you seek further help from the appropriate source.

Dog showing has been a very popular sport for a long time and has been taken quite seriously by some. Others only enjoy it as a hobby.

The Kennel Club in England was formed in 1859, the American Kennel Club was established in 1884 and the Canadian Kennel Club was formed in 1888. The purpose of these clubs was to register purebred dogs and maintain their Stud Books. In the beginning, the concept of registering dogs was not readily accepted. More than 36 million dogs have been enrolled in the AKC Stud Book since its inception in 1888. Presently the kennel clubs not only register dogs but adopt and enforce rules and regulations governing dog shows, obedience trials and field trials. Over the years they have fostered and encouraged interest in the health and welfare of the purebred dog. They routinely donate funds to veterinary research for study on genetic disorders.

Below are the addresses of the kennel clubs in the United States, Great Britain and Canada.

The American Kennel Club
260 Madison Avenue
New York, NY 10016
or 5580 Centerview Drive
Raleigh, NC 27606

The Kennel Club
1 Clarges Street

Picadilly, London, WIY 8AB, England

The Canadian Kennel Club
100-89 Skyway Avenue
Etobicoke, Ontario, Canada M9W 6R4

Today there are numerous activities that are enjoyable for both the dog and the handler. Some of the activities include conformation showing, obedience competition, tracking, agility, the Canine Good Citizen Certificate, and a wide range of instinct tests that vary from breed to breed. Where you start depends upon your goals which early on may not be readily apparent.

Whether you want your Westie pup to have a show career or you just want to introduce him to a new experience, puppy matches are a great place to begin.

CONFORMATION

Conformation showing is our oldest dog show sport. This type of showing is based on the dog's

appearance–that is his structure, movement and attitude. When considering this type of showing, you need to be aware of your breed's standard and be able to evaluate your dog compared to that standard. The breeder of your puppy or other experienced breeders would be good sources for such an evaluation. Puppies can go through lots of changes over a period of time. I always say most puppies start out as promising hopefuls and then after maturing may be disappointing as show candidates. Even so this should not deter them from being excellent pets.

Usually conformation training classes are offered by the local kennel or obedience clubs. These are excellent places for training puppies. The puppy should be able to walk on a lead before entering such a class. Proper ring procedure and technique for posing (stacking) the dog will be demonstrated as well as gaiting the dog. Usually certain patterns are used in the ring such as the triangle or the "L." Conformation class, like the PKT class, will give your youngster the opportunity to socialize with different breeds of dogs and humans too.

It takes some time to learn the routine of conformation showing. Usually one starts at the puppy matches which may be AKC Sanctioned or Fun Matches. These matches are generally for puppies from two or three months to a year old, and there may be classes for the adult over the age of 12 months. Similar to point shows, the classes are divided by sex and after completion of the classes in that breed or variety, the class winners compete for Best of Breed or Variety. The winner goes on to compete in the Group and the Group winners compete for Best in Match. No championship points are awarded for match wins.

A few matches can be great training for puppies even though there is no intention to go on showing. Matches enable the puppy to meet new people and be handled by a stranger–the judge. It

You can help your Westie learn the conformation show procedure by getting him accustomed to standing on a table. This is how he will be examined by the judges.

Corkey, owned by Lou Herczeg and Dawn Martin, is a truly versatile Westie. He is a conformation champion as well as the first Westie to obtain the Senior Earthdog title.

is also a change of environment, which broadens the horizon for both dog and handler. Matches and other dog activities boost the confidence of the handler and especially the younger handlers.

Earning an AKC championship is built on a point system, which is different from Great Britain. To become an AKC Champion of Record the dog must earn 15 points. The number of points earned each time depends upon the number of dogs in competition. The number of points available at each show depends upon the breed, its sex and the location of the show. The United States is divided into ten AKC zones. Each zone has its own set of points. The purpose of the zones is to try to equalize the points available from breed to breed and area to area.The AKC adjusts the point scale annually.

The number of points that can be won at a show are between one and five. Three-, four- and five-point wins are considered majors. Not only does the dog need 15 points won under three different judges, but those points must include two majors under two different judges. Canada also works on a point system but majors are not required.

Dogs always show before bitches. The classes available to those seeking points are: Puppy (which may be divided into 6 to 9 months and 9 to 12 months); 12 to 18 months; Novice; Bred-by-Exhibitor; American-bred; and Open. The class winners of the same sex of each breed or variety compete against each other for Winners Dog and Winners Bitch. A Reserve Winners Dog and Reserve Winners Bitch are also awarded but do not carry any points unless the Winners win is disallowed by AKC. The Winners Dog and Bitch compete with the specials (those dogs that have attained championship) for Best of Breed or Variety, Best of Winners and Best of Opposite Sex. It is possible to pick up an extra point or even a major if the points are higher for the defeated winner than those of Best of Winners. The latter would get the higher total from the defeated winner.

At an all-breed show, each Best of Breed or Variety winner will go on to his respective Group and then the Group winners will compete against each other for Best in Show. There are seven Groups: Sporting, Hounds, Working, Terriers, Toys, Non-Sporting and Herding. Obviously there are no Groups at speciality shows (those shows that have only one breed or a show such as the American Spaniel Club's Flushing Spaniel Show, which is for all flushing spaniel breeds).

Earning a championship in England is somewhat different

An-Van's Rough N Rowdy Rascal, JE, is a handsome highlander with promising conformation.

since they do not have a point system. Challenge Certificates are awarded if the judge feels the dog is deserving regardless of the number of dogs in competition. A dog must earn three Challenge Certificates under three different judges, with at least one of these Certificates being won after the age of 12 months. Competition is very strong and entries may be higher than they are in the U.S. The Kennel Club's Challenge Certificates are only available at Championship Shows.

Am.Can. Ch. Dawn's Up N' Adam, owned by the author, has earned Best in Show honors as well as his CDX and CG titles.

In England, The Kennel Club regulations require that certain dogs, Border Collies and Gundog breeds, qualify in a working capacity (i.e., obedience or field trials) before becoming a full Champion. If they do not qualify in the working aspect, then they are designated a Show Champion, which is equivalent to the AKC's Champion of Record. A Gundog may be granted the title of Field Trial Champion (FT Ch.) if it passes all the tests in the field but would also have to qualify in conformation before becoming a full Champion. A Border Collie that earns the title of Obedience Champion (Ob Ch.) must also qualify in the conformation ring before becoming a Champion.

The U.S. doesn't have a designation full Champion but does award for Dual and Triple Champions. The Dual Champion must be a Champion of Record, and either Champion Tracker, Herding Champion, Obedience Trial Champion or Field Champion. Any dog that has been awarded the titles of Champion of Record, and any two of the following: Champion Tracker, Herding Champion, Obedience Trial Champion or Field Champion, may be designated as a Triple Champion.

The shows in England seem to put more emphasis on breeder judges than those in the U.S. There is much competition within the breeds. Therefore the quality of the individual breeds should be very good. In the United States we tend to have more "all around judges" (those that judge multiple breeds) and use the breeder judges at the specialty shows. Breeder judges are more familiar with their own breed

since they are actively breeding that breed or did so at one time. Americans emphasize Group and Best in Show wins and promote them accordingly.

It is my understanding that the shows in England can be very large and extend over several days, with the Groups being scheduled on different days. I believe there is only one all-breed show in the U.S. that extends over two days, the Westminster Kennel Club Show. In our country we have cluster shows, where several different clubs will use the same show site over consecutive days.

Westminster Kennel Club is our most prestigious show although the entry is limited to 2500. In recent years, entry has been limited to Champions. This show is more formal than the majority of the shows with the judges wearing formal attire and the handlers fashionably dressed. In most instances the quality of the dogs is superb. After all, it is a show of Champions. It is a good show to study the AKC registered breeds and

Dog and handler alike must learn and adhere to the etiquette of the conformation show ring.

is by far the most exciting—especially since it is televised! WKC is one of the few shows in this country that is still benched. This means the dog must be in his benched area during the show hours except when he is being groomed, in the ring, or being exercised.

Typically, the handlers are very particular about their appearances. They are careful not to wear something that will detract from their dog but will perhaps enhance it. American ring procedure is quite formal compared to that of other countries. I remember being reprimanded by a judge because I made a suggestion to a friend holding my second dog outside the ring. I certainly could have used more discretion so I would not call attention to myself. There is a certain etiquette expected between the judge and exhibitor and among the other exhibitors. Of course it is not always the case but the judge is supposed to be polite, not

A Westie must patiently stand while his handler poses him and the judge evaluates his conformation.

engaging in small talk or even acknowledging that he knows the handler. I understand that there is a more informal and relaxed atmosphere at the shows in other countries. For instance, the dress code is more casual. I can see where this might be more fun for the exhibitor and especially for the novice. This country is very handler-oriented in many of the breeds. It is true, in most instances, that the experienced professional handler can present the dog better and will have a feel for what a judge likes.

In England, Crufts is The Kennel Club's own show and is most assuredly the largest dog show in the world. They've been known to have an entry of nearly 20,000, and the show lasts four days. Entry is only gained by qualifying through winning in specified classes at another Championship Show. Westminster is strictly conformation, but Crufts exhibitors and spectators enjoy not only conformation but obedience, agility and a multitude of exhibitions as well. Obedience was admitted in 1957 and agility in 1983.

If you are handling your own dog, please give some consideration to your apparel. For sure the dress code at matches is more informal than the point shows. However, you should wear something a little more appropriate than beach attire or ragged jeans and bare feet. If you check out the handlers and see what is presently fashionable, you'll catch on. Men usually dress with a shirt and tie and a nice sports coat. Whether you are male or female, you will want to wear comfortable clothes and shoes. You need to be able to run with your dog and you certainly don't want to take a chance of falling and hurting yourself. Heaven forbid, if nothing else, you'll upset your dog. Women usually wear a dress or two-piece outfit, preferably with pockets to carry bait, comb, brush, etc. In this case men are the lucky ones with all their pockets. Ladies, think about where your dress will be if you need to kneel on the floor and also think about running. Does it allow freedom to do so?

Years ago, after toting around all the baby paraphernalia, I found toting the dog and necessities a breeze. You need to take along dog; crate; ex pen (if you use one); extra newspaper; water pail and water; all required grooming equipment, including hair dryer and extension cord; table; chair for you; bait for dog and lunch for you and friends; and, last but not least, clean up materials, such as plastic bags, paper towels, and perhaps a bath towel and some shampoo—just in case. Don't forget your entry confirmation and directions to the show.

If you are showing in obedience, then you will want to wear pants. Many of our top obedience handlers wear pants that are color-coordinated with their dogs. The philosophy is that imperfections in the black dog will be less obvious next to your black pants.

Whether you are showing in conformation, Junior Showmanship or obedience, you need to watch the clock and be sure you are not late. It is customary to pick up your conformation armband a few minutes before the start of the class. They will not wait for you and if you are on the show grounds and not in the ring, you will upset everyone. It's a little more complicated picking up your obedience armband if you show later in the class. If you have not picked up your armband and they get to your number, you may not be allowed to show. It's best to pick up your armband early, but then you may show earlier than expected if other handlers don't pick up. Customarily all conflicts should be discussed with the judge prior to the start of the class.

Successful showing requires dedication and preparation, but most of all, it should be an enjoyable experience for you and your Westie.

Junior Showmanship

The Junior Showmanship Class is a wonderful way to build self confidence even if there are no aspirations of staying with the dog-show game later in life. Frequently, Junior Showmanship becomes the background of those who become successful exhibitors/handlers in the future. In some instances

Canine Good Citizens must be able to get along with other dogs—these affectionate Westie pups have passed the test!

it is taken very seriously, and success is measured in terms of wins. The Junior Handler is judged solely on his ability and skill in presenting his dog. The dog's conformation is not to be considered by the judge. Even so the condition and grooming of the dog may be a reflection upon the handler.

Usually the matches and point shows include different classes. The Junior Handler's dog may be entered in a breed or obedience class and even shown by another person in that class. Junior Showmanship classes are usually divided by age and perhaps sex. The age is determined by the handler's age on the day of the show. The classes are:

Novice Junior for those at least ten and under 14 years of age who at time of entry closing have not won three first places in a Novice Class at a licensed or member show.

Novice Senior for those at least 14 and under 18 years of age who at the time of entry closing have not won three first places in a Novice Class at a licensed or member show.

Open Junior for those at least ten and under 14 years of age who at the time of entry closing have won at least three first places in a Novice Junior Showmanship Class at a licensed or member show with competition present.

Open Senior for those at least 14 and under 18 years of age who at time of entry closing have won at least three first places in a Novice Junior Showmanship Class at a licensed or member show with competition present.

Junior Handlers must include their AKC Junior Handler number on each show entry. This needs to be obtained from the AKC.

CANINE GOOD CITIZEN

The AKC sponsors a program to encourage dog owners to train their dogs. Local clubs perform the pass/fail tests, and dogs who pass are awarded a Canine Good Citizen Certificate. Proof of vaccination is required at the time of participation. The test includes:

Everyone should have a dog as friendly as this Westie! The Canine Good Citizen Test encourages people to train and socialize their dogs.

1. Accepting a friendly stranger.
2. Sitting politely for petting.
3. Appearance and grooming.
4. Walking on a loose leash.
5. Walking through a crowd.
6. Sit and down on command/staying in place.
7. Come when called.
8. Reaction to another dog.
9. Reactions to distractions.
10. Supervised separation.

If more effort was made by pet owners to accomplish these exercises, fewer dogs would be cast off to the humane shelter.

OBEDIENCE

Obedience is necessary, without a doubt, but it can also

become a wonderful hobby or even an obsession. In my opinion, obedience classes and competition can provide wonderful companionship, not only with your dog but with your classmates or fellow competitors. It is always gratifying to discuss your dog's problems with others who have had similar experiences. The AKC acknowledged Obedience around 1936, and it has changed tremendously even though many of the exercises are basically the same. Today, obedience competition is just that—very competitive. Even so, it is possible for every obedience exhibitor to come home a winner (by earning qualifying scores) even though he/she may not earn a placement in the class.

Most of the obedience titles are awarded after earning three qualifying scores (legs) in the appropriate class under three different judges. These classes offer a perfect score of 200, which is extremely rare. Each of the class exercises has its own point value. A leg is earned after receiving a score of at least 170 and at least 50 percent of the points available in each exercise. The titles are:

Companion Dog—CD

This is called the Novice Class and the exercises are:

1. Heel on leash and figure 8	40 points
2. Stand for examination	30 points
3. Heel free	40 points
4. Recall	30 points
5. Long sit—one minute	30 points
6. Long down—three minutes	30 points
Maximum total score	200 points

Companion Dog Excellent—CDX

This is the Open Class and the exercises are:

1. Heel off leash and figure 8	40 points
2. Drop on recall	30 points
3. Retrieve on flat	20 points
4. Retrieve over high jump	30 points
5. Broad jump	20 points
6. Long sit—three minutes (out of sight)	30 points
7. Long down—five minutes (out of sight)	30 points
Maximum total score	200 points

Utility Dog–UD

The Utility Class exercises are:

1. Signal Exercise	40 points
2. Scent discrimination–Article 1	30 points
3. Scent discrimination–Article 2	30 points
4. Directed retrieve	30 points
5. Moving stand and examination	30 points
6. Directed jumping	40 points
Maximum total score	200 points

After achieving the UD title, you may feel inclined to go after the UDX and/or OTCh. The UDX (Utility Dog Excellent) title went into effect in January 1994. It is not easily attained. The title requires qualifying simultaneously ten times in Open B and Utility B but not necessarily at consecutive shows.

Obedience competition requires concentration and focus on the part of handler and dog...hey, are you paying attention?

The OTCh (Obedience Trial Champion) is awarded after the dog has earned his UD and then goes on to earn

100 championship points, a first place in Utility, a first place in Open and another first place in either class. The placements must be won under three different judges at all-breed obedience trials. The points are determined by the number of dogs competing in the Open B and Utility B classes. The OTCh title precedes the dog's name.

Obedience matches (AKC Sanctioned, Fun, and Show and Go) are usually available. Usually they are sponsored by the local obedience clubs. When preparing an obedience dog for a title, you will find matches very helpful. Fun Matches and Show and Go Matches are more lenient in allowing you to make corrections in the ring. I frequently train (correct) in the ring and inform the judge that I would like to do so and to please mark me "exhibition." This means that I will not be eligible for any prize. This type of training is usually very necessary for the Open and Utility Classes. AKC Sanctioned Obedience Matches do not allow corrections in the ring since they must abide by the AKC Obedience Regulations. If you are interested in

The directed retrieve is one of the exercises in the Utility Class.

showing in obedience, then you should contact the AKC for a copy of the Obedience Regulations.

GENERAL INFORMATION

Obedience, tracking and agility allow the purebred dog with an Indefinite Listing Privilege (ILP) number or a limited registration to be exhibited and earn titles. Application must be made to the AKC for an ILP number.

The American Kennel Club publishes a monthly *Events* magazine that is part of the *Gazette*, their official journal for the sport of purebred dogs. The *Events* section lists upcoming shows and the secretary or superintendent for them. The majority of the conformation shows in the U.S. are overseen by licensed superintendents. Generally the entry closing date is approximately two-and-a-half weeks before the actual show. Point shows are fairly expensive, while the match shows cost about one third of the point show entry fee. Match shows usually take entries the day of the show but some are pre-entry. The best way to find match show information is through your local kennel club. Upon asking, the AKC can provide you with a list of superintendents, and you can write and ask to be put on their mailing lists.

Westies are well suited to all types of activities and are successful in many different areas of dog competition. Have fun discovering where your Westie's talent lies!

Obedience trial and tracking test information is available through the AKC. Frequently these events are not superintended, but put on by the host club. Therefore you would make the entry with the event's secretary.

As you have read, there are numerous activities you can share with your dog. Regardless what you do, it does take teamwork. Your dog can only benefit from your attention and training. I hope this chapter has enlightened you and hope, if nothing else, you will attend a show here and there. Perhaps you will start with a puppy kindergarten class, and who knows where it may lead!

HEALTH CARE

V eterinary medicine has become far more sophisticated than what was available to our ancestors. This can be attributed to the increase in household pets and consequently the demand for better care for them. Also human medicine has become far more complex. Today diagnostic testing in veterinary medicine parallels human diagnostics. Because of better technology we can expect our pets to live healthier lives thereby increasing their life spans.

THE FIRST CHECK UP

You will want to take your new puppy/dog in for its first check up within 48 to 72 hours after acquiring it. Many breeders strongly recommend this check up and so do the humane shelters. A

Your Westie's health is important from day one. One-day-old Amelia is owned by Stephanie Capkovic.

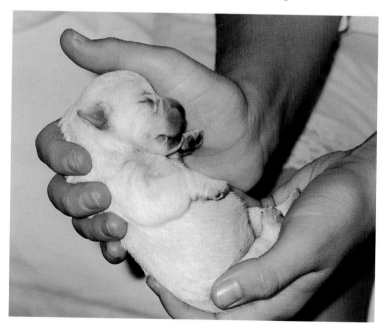

It is possible for a dog or puppy to appear healthy, yet have a serious medical condition. Regular visits to the veterinarian will help detect any underlying problems.

puppy/dog can appear healthy but it may have a serious problem that is not apparent to the layman. Most pets have some type of a minor flaw that may never cause a real problem.

Unfortunately if he/she should have a serious problem, you will want to consider the consequences of keeping the pet and the attachments that will be formed, which may be broken prematurely. Keep in mind there are many healthy dogs looking for good homes.

This first check up is a good time to establish yourself with the veterinarian and learn the office policy regarding their hours and how they handle emergencies. Usually the breeder or another conscientious pet owner is a good reference for locating a capable veterinarian. You should be aware that not all veterinarians give the same quality of service. Please do not make your selection on the least expensive clinic, as they may be short changing your pet. There is the possibility that eventually it will cost you more due to improper diagnosis, treatment, etc. If you are selecting a new veterinarian, feel free to ask for a tour of the clinic. You should inquire about making an appointment for a tour since all clinics are working clinics, and therefore may not be available all day for sightseers. You may worry less if you see where your pet will be spending the day if he ever needs to be hospitalized.

THE PHYSICAL EXAM

Your veterinarian will check your pet's overall condition, which includes listening to the heart; checking the respiration; feeling the abdomen, muscles and joints; checking the mouth, which includes the gum color and signs of gum disease along with plaque buildup; checking the ears for signs of an infection or ear mites; examining the eyes; and, last but not least, checking the condition of the skin and coat.

Your Westie's physical exam will include a thorough inspection of his mouth, teeth, and gums.

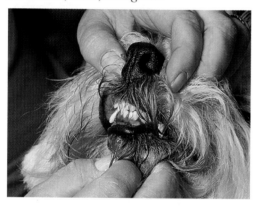

He should ask you questions regarding your pet's eating and elimination habits and invite you to relay your questions. It is a good idea to prepare a list so as not to forget anything. He should discuss the proper diet and the quantity to be fed. If this should differ from your breeder's recommendation, then you should convey to him the breeder's choice and see if he approves. If he recommends changing the diet, then this should be done over a few days so as not to cause a gastrointestinal upset. It is customary to take in a fresh stool sample (just a small amount) for a test for intestinal parasites. It must be fresh, preferably within 12 hours, since the eggs hatch quickly and after hatching will not be observed under the microscope. If your pet isn't obliging then, usually the technician can take one in the clinic.

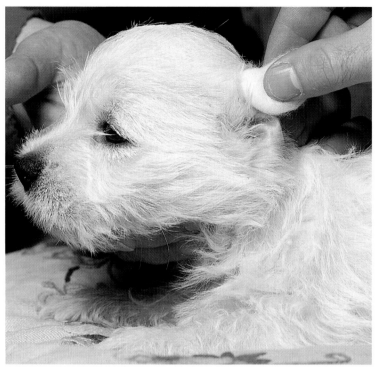

The veterinarian will check your Westie's ears for any evidence of infection or ear mite infestation.

IMMUNIZATIONS

It is important that you take your puppy/dog's vaccination record with you on your first visit. In case of a puppy, presumably the breeder has seen to the vaccinations up to the time you acquired custody. Veterinarians differ in their vaccination protocol. It is not unusual for your puppy to have received vaccinations for distemper, hepatitis, leptospirosis, parvovirus and parainfluenza every two to three weeks from the age of five or six weeks. Usually this is a combined injection and is typically called the DHLPP. The DHLPP is given through at least 12 to 14 weeks of age, and it is customary to continue with another parvovirus vaccine at 16 to 18 weeks. You may wonder why so many immunizations are necessary. No one knows for sure when the puppy's maternal antibodies are gone, although it is customarily accepted that distemper antibodies are gone by 12 weeks. Usually parvovirus antibodies are gone by 16 to 18 weeks of age. However, it is possible for the maternal antibodies to be gone at a much earlier age or even a later age. Therefore immunizations are started at an early age. The vaccine will not give immunity as long as there are maternal antibodies.

The rabies vaccination is given at three or six months of age depending on your local laws. A vaccine for bordetella (kennel cough) is advisable and can be given anytime from the age of five weeks. The coronavirus is not commonly given unless there is a problem locally. The Lyme vaccine is necessary in endemic areas. Lyme disease has been reported in 47 states.

Distemper

This is virtually an incurable disease. If the dog recovers, he is subject to severe nervous disorders. The virus attacks every tissue in the body and resembles a bad cold with a fever. It can cause a runny nose and eyes and cause gastrointestinal disorders, including a poor appetite, vomiting and diarrhea. The virus is carried by raccoons, foxes, wolves, mink and other dogs. Unvaccinated youngsters and senior citizens are very susceptible. This is still a common disease.

Hepatitis

This is a virus that is most serious in very young dogs. It is spread by contact with an infected animal or its stool or urine. The virus affects the liver and kidneys and is characterized by high fever, depression and lack of appetite. Recovered animals may be afflicted with chronic illnesses.

Bordetella attached to canine cilia. Otherwise known as kennel cough, this disease is highly contagious and should be vaccinated against routinely.

Leptospirosis

This is a bacterial disease transmitted by contact with the urine of an infected dog, rat or other wildlife. It produces severe symptoms of fever, depression, jaundice and internal bleeding and was fatal before the vaccine was developed. Recovered dogs can be carriers, and the disease can be transmitted from dogs to humans.

Parvovirus

This was first noted in the late 1970s and is still a fatal disease. However, with proper vaccinations, early diagnosis and prompt treatment, it is a manageable

Pups should be kept with their littermates and only handled by the breeder until they are properly vaccinated. Socializing pups too early can lead to the spread of disease.

disease. It attacks the bone marrow and intestinal tract. The symptoms include depression, loss of appetite, vomiting, diarrhea and collapse. Immediate medical attention is of the essence.

Rabies

This is shed in the saliva and is carried by raccoons, skunks, foxes, other dogs and cats. It attacks nerve tissue, resulting in paralysis and death. Rabies can be transmitted to people and is virtually always fatal. This disease is reappearing in the suburbs.

Bordetella (Kennel Cough)

The symptoms are coughing, sneezing, hacking and retching accompanied by nasal discharge usually lasting from a few days to several weeks. There are several disease-producing organisms responsible for this disease. The present vaccines are helpful but do not protect for all the strains. It usually is not life threatening but in some instances it can progress to a serious bronchopneumonia. The disease is highly contagious. The vaccination should be given routinely for dogs that come in contact with other dogs, such as through boarding, training class or visits to the groomer.

Coronavirus

This is usually self limiting and not life threatening. It was first noted in the late '70s about a year before parvovirus. The virus produces a yellow/brown stool and there may be depression, vomiting and diarrhea.

Regular medical care is as important for the adult Westie as it is for the pup. Routine tests, booster vaccinations, and physical exams are part of your dog's lifelong maintenance.

Lyme Disease

This was first diagnosed in the United States in 1976 in Lyme, CT in people who lived in close proximity to the deer tick. Symptoms may include acute lameness, fever, swelling of joints and loss of appetite. Your veterinarian can advise you if you live in an endemic area.

After your puppy has completed his puppy vaccinations, you will continue to booster the DHLPP once a year. It is customary to booster the rabies one year after the first vaccine and then, depending on where you live, it should be boostered every year or every three years. This depends on your local laws. The Lyme and corona vaccines are boostered annually and it is recommended that the bordetella be boostered every six to eight months.

ANNUAL VISIT

I would like to impress the importance of the annual check up, which would include the booster vaccinations, check for intestinal parasites and test for heartworm. Today in our very busy world it is rush, rush and see "how much you can get for how little." Unbelievably, some non-veterinary businesses have entered into the vaccination business. More harm than good can come to your dog through improper vaccinations, possibly from inferior vaccines and/or the wrong schedule. More than likely you truly care about your companion dog and over the years you have devoted much time and expense to his well being. Perhaps you

The deer tick is the most common carrier of Lyme disease. Photo courtesy of Virbac Laboratories, Inc., Fort Worth, Texas.

are unaware that a vaccination is not just a vaccination. There is more involved. Please, please follow through with regular physical examinations. It is so important for your veterinarian to know your dog and this is especially true during middle age through the geriatric years. More than likely your older dog will require more than one physical a year. The annual physical is good preventive medicine. Through early diagnosis and subsequent treatment your dog can maintain a longer and better quality of life.

INTESTINAL PARASITES

Hookworms

These are almost microscopic intestinal worms that can cause anemia and therefore serious problems, including death, in young puppies. Hookworms can be transmitted to humans through penetration of the skin. Puppies may be born with them.

Hookworms are almost microscopic intestinal worms that can cause anemia and therefore serious problems, including death.

Roundworms

These are spaghetti-like worms that

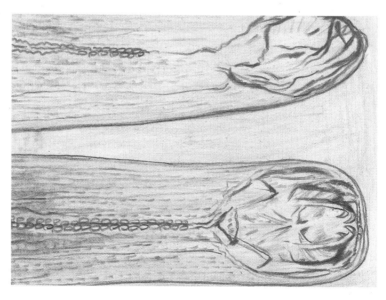

can cause a potbellied appearance and dull coat along with more severe symptoms, such as vomiting, diarrhea and coughing. Puppies acquire these while in the mother's uterus and through lactation. Both hookworms and roundworms may be acquired through ingestion.

Whipworms

These have a three-month life cycle and are not acquired through the dam. They cause intermittent diarrhea usually with mucus. Whipworms are possibly the most difficult worm to eradicate. Their eggs are very resistant to most environmental factors and can last for years until the proper conditions enable them to mature. Whipworms are seldom seen in the stool.

Roundworm eggs, as would be seen on a fecal evaluation. The eggs must develop for at least 12 days before they are infective.

Intestinal parasites are more prevalent in some areas than others. Climate, soil and contamination are big factors contributing to the incidence of intestinal parasites. Eggs are passed in the stool, lay on the ground and then become infective in a certain number of days. Each of the above worms has a different life cycle. Your best chance of becoming and remaining worm-free is to always pooper-scoop your yard. A fenced-in yard keeps stray dogs out, which is certainly helpful.

I would recommend having a fecal examination on your dog twice a year or more often if there is a problem. If your dog has a positive fecal sample, then he will be given the appropriate medication and you will be asked to bring back another stool sample in a certain period of time (depending on the type of worm) and then be rewormed. This process goes on until he has at least two negative samples. The different types of worms require different medications. You will be wasting your money and doing your dog an injustice by buying over-the-counter medication without first consulting your veterinarian.

OTHER INTERNAL PARASITES

Coccidiosis and Giardiasis

These protozoal infections usually affect puppies, especially in places where large numbers of puppies are brought together. Older dogs may harbor these infections but do not show signs unless they are stressed. Symptoms include diarrhea, weight loss and lack of appetite. These infections are not always apparent in the fecal examination.

Tapeworms

Seldom apparent on fecal floatation, they are diagnosed frequently as rice-like segments around the dog's anus and the base of the tail. Tapeworms are long, flat and ribbon like, sometimes several feet in length, and made up of many segments about five-eighths of an inch long. The two most common types of tapeworms found in the dog are:

(1) First the larval form of the flea tapeworm parasite must mature in an intermediate host, the flea, before it can become infective. Your dog acquires this by ingesting the flea through licking and chewing.

(2) Rabbits, rodents and certain large game animals serve as intermediate hosts for other species of tapeworms. If your dog should eat one of these infected hosts, then he can acquire tapeworms.

Heartworm Disease

This is a worm that resides in the heart and adjacent blood vessels of the lung that produces microfilaria, which circulate in the bloodstream. It is possible for a dog to be infected with any number of worms from one to a hundred that can be 6 to 14 inches long. It is a life-threatening disease, expensive to treat and easily prevented. Depending on where you live, your veterinarian may recommend a preventive year-round and either an annual or semiannual blood test. The most common preventive is given once a month.

External Parasites

Ticks

Ticks carry Rocky Mountain Spotted Fever, Lyme disease and can cause tick paralysis. They should be removed with tweezers, trying to pull out the head. The jaws carry disease. There is a tick preventive collar that does an excellent job. The ticks automatically back out on those dogs wearing collars.

Sarcoptic Mange

This is a mite that is difficult to find on skin scrapings. The pinnal reflex is a good indicator of this disease. Rub the ends of the pinna (ear) together and the dog will start scratching with his foot. Sarcoptes are highly contagious to other dogs and to humans although they do not live long on humans. They cause intense itching.

Demodectic Mange

This is a mite that is passed from the dam to her puppies. It affects youngsters age three to ten months. Diagnosis is confirmed by skin scraping. Small areas of alopecia around the eyes, lips and/ or forelegs become visible. There is little itching unless there is a secondary bacterial infection. Some breeds are afflicted more than others.

Ticks are carriers of diseases that are easily spread to dogs and humans. Thoroughly inspect your Westie for ticks, especially if he has been playing in a wooded or grassy area.

Cheyletiella

This causes intense itching and is diagnosed by skin scraping. It lives in the outer layers of the skin of dogs, cats, rabbits and humans. Yellow-gray scales may be found on the back and the rump, top of the head and the nose.

TO BREED OR NOT TO BREED

More than likely your breeder has requested that you have your puppy neutered or spayed. Your breeder's request is based on what is healthiest for your dog and what is most beneficial for your breed. Experienced and conscientious breeders devote many years into developing a bloodline. In order to do this, he makes every effort to plan each breeding in regard to conformation, temperament and health. This type of breeder does his best to perform the necessary testing (i.e., OFA, CERF, testing for inherited blood disorders, thyroid, etc.). Testing is expensive and sometimes very disheartening when a favorite dog doesn't pass his health tests. The health history pertains not only to the breeding stock but to the immediate ancestors. Reputable breeders do not want their offspring to be bred indiscriminately. Therefore you may be asked to neuter or spay your puppy. Of course there is always the exception, and your breeder may agree to let you breed your dog under his direct supervision. This is an important concept. More and more effort is being made to breed healthier dogs.

Spay/Neuter

There are numerous benefits of performing this surgery at six months of age. Unspayed females are subject to mammary

Cute Westie pups can be irresistible—but do you have the time and energy to care for a litter? This is just one point to ponder in making the decision to spay/ neuter.

and ovarian cancer. In order to prevent mammary cancer she must be spayed prior to her first heat cycle. Later in life, an unspayed female may develop a pyometra (an infected uterus), which is definitely life threatening.

Spaying is performed under a general anesthetic and is easy on the young dog. As you might expect it is a little harder on the older dog, but that is no reason to deny her the surgery. The surgery removes the ovaries and uterus. It is important to remove all the ovarian

Having your Westie spayed or neutered will minimize his risk of many health problems, including certain cancers of the reproductive organs.

Ch. Dawn's Kop N' A Plea, SE, and her brood. Only dogs that can contribute to the well-being and consistency of the breed should be used in breeding programs.

tissue. If some is left behind, she could remain attractive to males. In order to view the ovaries, a reasonably long incision is necessary. An ovariohysterectomy is considered major surgery.

Neutering the male at a young age will inhibit some characteristic male behavior that owners frown upon. I have found my boys will not hike their legs and mark territory if they are neutered at six months of age. Also neutering at a young age has hormonal benefits, lessening the chance of hormonal aggressiveness.

A conscientious breeder will often sell puppies that he feels should not be bred with the stipulation that the new owners have the pups spayed or neutered.

Surgery involves removing the testicles but leaving the scrotum. If there should be a retained testicle, then he definitely needs to be neutered before the age of two or three years. Retained testicles can develop into cancer. Unneutered males are at risk for testicular cancer, perineal fistulas, perianal tumors and fistulas and prostatic disease.

Intact males and females are prone to housebreaking accidents. Females urinate frequently before, during and after heat cycles, and males tend to mark territory if there is a female in heat. Males may show the same behavior if there is a visiting dog or guests.

Surgery involves a sterile operating procedure equivalent to human surgery. The incision site is shaved, surgically scrubbed and draped. The veterinarian wears a sterile surgical gown, cap, mask and gloves. Anesthesia should be monitored by a registered technician. It is customary for the veterinarian to recommend a pre-anesthetic blood screening, looking for metabolic problems and a ECG rhythm strip to check for normal heart function. Today anesthetics are equal to human anesthetics, which enables your dog to walk out of the clinic the same day as surgery.

Some folks worry about their dog gaining weight after being neutered or spayed. This is usually not the case. It is true that some dogs may be less active so they could develop a problem, but my own dogs are just as active as they were before surgery. I have a hard time keeping weight on them. However, if your dog should begin to gain, then you need to decrease his food and see to it that he gets a little more exercise.

DENTAL CARE for Your Dog's Life

So you've got a new puppy! You also have a new set of puppy teeth in your household. Anyone who has ever raised a puppy is abundantly aware of these new teeth. Your puppy will chew anything it can reach, chase your shoelaces, and play "tear the rag" with any piece of clothing it can find. When puppies are newly born, they have no teeth. At about four weeks of age, puppies of most breeds begin to develop their deciduous or baby teeth. They begin eating semi-solid food, fighting and biting with their litter mates, and learning discipline from their mother. As their new teeth come in, they inflict more pain on their mother's breasts, so her feeding sessions become less frequent and shorter. By six or eight weeks, the mother will start growling to warn her pups when they are fighting too roughly or hurting her as they nurse too much with their new teeth.

Puppies need to chew. It is a necessary part of their physical and mental development. They develop muscles and necessary life skills as they drag objects around, fight over possession, and vocalize alerts and warnings. Puppies chew on things to explore their world. They are using their sense of taste to determine what is food and what is not. How else can they tell an electrical cord from a lizard? At about four months of age, most puppies begin shedding their baby teeth. Often these teeth need some help to come out and make way for the permanent teeth. The incisors (front teeth) will be replaced first. Then, the adult canine or fang teeth erupt. When the baby tooth is not shed before

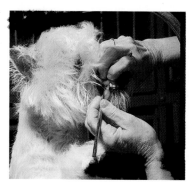

Your veterinarian will inspect your Westie's mouth as part of his physical exam, but you should take an active part in your dog's preventive oral health care.

Quality chew toys play a big role in the proper development of a puppy's permanent teeth. Nylafloss® is great for puppies as it aids in the removal of baby teeth and is fun, too.

the permanent tooth comes in, veterinarians call it a retained deciduous tooth. This condition will often cause gum infections by trapping hair and debris between the permanent tooth and the retained baby tooth. Nylafloss® is an excellent device for puppies to use. They can toss it, drag it, and chew on the many surfaces it presents. The baby teeth can catch in the nylon material, aiding in their removal. Puppies that have adequate chew toys will have less destructive behavior, develop more physically, and have less chance of retained deciduous teeth.

During the first year, your dog should be seen by your veterinarian at regular intervals. Your veterinarian will let you know when to bring in your puppy for vaccinations and parasite examinations. At each visit, your veterinarian should inspect the lips, teeth, and mouth as part of a complete physical examination. You should take some part in the maintenance of your dog's oral health. You should examine your dog's mouth weekly throughout his first year to make

sure there are no sores, foreign objects, tooth problems, etc. If your dog drools excessively, shakes its head, or has bad breath, consult your veterinarian. By the time your dog is six months old, the permanent teeth are all in and plaque can start to accumulate on the tooth surfaces. This is when your dog needs to develop good dental-care habits to prevent calculus build-up on its teeth. Brushing is best. That is a fact that cannot be denied. However, some dogs do not like their teeth brushed regularly, or you may not be able to accomplish the task. In that case, you should consider a product that will help prevent plaque and calculus build-up.

A relaxing afternoon in the cool grass with his favorite Nylabone®— what more could a Westie ask for?

The Dental Chews and Galileo Bone® are other excellent choices for the first three years of a dog's life. Their shapes make them interesting for the dog. As the dog chews on them, the solid polyurethane massages the gums which improves the blood circulation to the periodontal tissues. Projections on the chew devices increase the surface and are in contact with the tooth for more efficient cleaning. The unique shape and consistency prevent your dog from exerting excessive force on his own teeth or from breaking off pieces of the bone. If your dog is an aggressive chewer or weighs more than 55 pounds (25 kg), you should consider giving him a Nylabone®, the most durable chew product on the market.

The Nylabone® Flexible, made by the Nylabone Company, is constructed of strong polyurethane, which is softer than nylon. Less powerful chewers prefer the Nylabone® Flexible to the Nylabone®. A super option for your dog is the Hercules Bone®,

Dental Chews have raised dental tips that massage the dog's gums and clean the dog's teeth as he chews. Their shapes are appealing to dogs—this Westie thinks so!

a uniquely shaped bone named after the great Olympian for its exceptional strength. Like all Nylabone products, they are specially scented to make them attractive to your dog. Ask your veterinarian about these bones and he will validate the good doctor's prescription: Nylabones® not only give your dog a good chewing workout but also help to save your dog's teeth (and even his life, as it protects him from possible fatal periodontal diseases).

By the time dogs are four years old, 75% of them have periodontal disease. It is the most common infection in dogs. Yearly examinations by your veterinarian are essential to maintaining your dog's good health. If your veterinarian detects periodontal disease, he or she may recommend a prophylactic cleaning. To do a thorough cleaning, it will be necessary to put your dog under anesthesia. With modern gas anesthetics and monitoring equipment, the procedure is pretty safe. Your veterinarian will scale the teeth with an ultrasound scaler or hand instrument. This removes the calculus from the teeth. If there are calculus deposits below the gum line, the veterinarian will plane the roots to make them smooth. After all of the calculus has been removed, the teeth are polished with pumice in a polishing cup. If any medical or surgical treatment is needed, it is done at this time. The final step would be fluoride treatment and your follow-up treatment at home. If the periodontal disease is advanced, the veterinarian may prescribe a medicated mouth rinse or antibiotics for use at home. Make sure your dog has safe, clean and attractive chew toys and treats. Chooz® treats are another way of using a

Providing your Westie with nutritious treats will help keep him fit. Some treats also help keep his teeth clean.

consumable treat to help keep your dog's teeth clean.

Rawhide is the most popular of all materials for a dog to chew. This has never been good news to dog owners, because rawhide is inherently very dangerous for dogs. Thousands of dogs have died from rawhide, having swallowed the hide after it has become soft and mushy, only to cause stomach and intestinal blockage. A new rawhide product on the market has finally solved the problem of rawhide: molded Roar-Hide® from Nylabone®. These are composed of processed, cut up, and melted American rawhide injected into your dog's favorite shape: a dog bone. These dog-safe devices smell and taste like rawhide but don't break up. The ridges on the bones help to fight tartar build-up on the teeth and they last ten times longer than the usual rawhide chews.

A Dental Chew that's half his size is a little bit overwhelming for this Westie pup— luckily, they come in small sizes for small dogs, too.

As your dog ages, professional examination and cleaning should become more frequent. The mouth should be inspected at least once a year. Your veterinarian may recommend visits every six months. In the geriatric patient, organs such as the heart, liver, and kidneys do not function as well as when they were young. Your veterinarian will probably want to test these organs' functions prior to using general anesthesia for dental cleaning. If your dog is a good chewer and you work closely with your veterinarian, your dog can keep all of its teeth all of its life. However, as your dog ages, his sense of smell, sight, and taste will diminish. He may not have the desire to chase, trap or chew his toys. He will also not have the energy to chew for long periods, as arthritis and periodontal disease make chewing painful. This will leave you with more responsibility for keeping his teeth clean and healthy. The dog that would not let you brush his teeth at one year of age, may let you brush his teeth now that he is ten years old.

If you train your dog with good chewing habits as a puppy, he will have healthier teeth throughout his life.

IDENTIFICATION and Finding the Lost Dog

There are several ways of identifying your dog. The old standby is a collar with dog license, rabies, and ID tags. Unfortunately collars have a way of being separated from the dog and tags fall off. I am not suggesting you shouldn't use a collar and tags. If they stay intact and on the dog, they are the quickest way of identification.

For several years owners have been tattooing their dogs. Some tattoos use a number with a registry. Here lies the problem because there are several registries to check. If you wish to tattoo, use your social security number. The humane

The newest method of identification is microchipping. The microchip is a computer chip that is no bigger than a grain of rice.

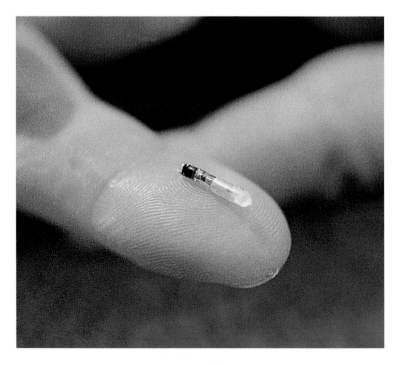

A fence is a good safety precaution, but it is not a guarantee that your dog will stay in the yard. Always supervise your Westie when he is off lead, even in a fenced-in area.

shelters have the means to trace it. It is usually done on the inside of the rear thigh. The area is first shaved and numbed. There is no pain, although a few dogs do not like the buzzing sound. Occasionally tattooing is not legible and needs to be redone.

The newest method of identification is microchipping. The microchip is a computer chip that is no larger than a grain of rice. The veterinarian implants it by injection between the shoulder blades. The dog feels no discomfort. If your dog is lost and picked up by the humane society, they can trace you by scanning the microchip, which has its own code. Microchip scanners are friendly to other brands of microchips and their registries. The microchip comes with a dog tag saying the dog is microchipped. It is the safest way of identifying your dog.

FINDING THE LOST DOG

I am sure you will agree with me that there would be little worse than losing your dog. Responsible pet owners rarely lose their dogs. They do not let their dogs run free because they don't want harm to come to them. Not only that but in most, if not all, states there is a leash law.

Beware of fenced-in yards. They can be a hazard. Dogs find ways to escape either over or under the fence. Another fast exit is through the gate that perhaps the neighbor's child left unlocked.

It is always helpful to have a good, clear picture of your Westie. Should he get lost, you can put his picture on flyers in the hope that someone will recognize him.

Below is a list that hopefully will be of help to you if you need it. Remember don't give up, keep looking. Your dog is worth your efforts.

1. Contact your neighbors and put flyers with a photo on it in their mailboxes. Information you should include would be the dog's name, breed, sex, color, age, source of identification, when your dog was last seen and where, and your name and phone numbers. It may be helpful to say the dog needs medical care. Offer a *reward*.
2. Check all local shelters daily. It is also possible for your dog to be picked up away from home and end up in an out-of-the-way shelter. Check these too. Go in person. It is not good enough to call. Most shelters are limited on the time they can hold dogs then they are put up for adoption or euthanized. There is the possibility that your dog will not make it to the shelter for several days. Your dog could have been wandering or someone may have tried to keep him.
3. Notify all local veterinarians. Call and send flyers.
4. Call your breeder. Frequently breeders are contacted when one of their breed is found.
5. Contact the rescue group for your breed.
6. Contact local schools—children may have seen your dog.
7. Post flyers at the schools, groceries, gas stations, convenience stores, veterinary clinics, groomers and any other place that will allow them.
8. Advertise in the newspaper.
9. Advertise on the radio.

TRAVELING with Your Dog

The earlier you start traveling with your new puppy or dog, the better. He needs to become accustomed to traveling. However, some dogs are nervous riders and become carsick easily. It is helpful if he starts with an empty stomach. Do not despair, as it will go better if you continue taking him with you on short fun rides. How would you feel if every time you rode in the car you stopped at the doctor's for an injection? You would soon dread that nasty car. Older dogs that tend to get carsick may have more of a problem adjusting to traveling. Those dogs that are having a serious problem may benefit from some medication prescribed by the veterinarian.

Do give your dog a chance to relieve himself before getting into the car. It is a good idea to be prepared for a clean up with a leash, paper towels, bag and terry cloth towel.

The safest place for your dog is in a fiberglass crate, although close confinement can promote carsickness in some dogs. If your dog is nervous you can try letting him ride on the seat next to you or in someone's lap.

An alternative to the crate would be to use a car harness made for dogs and/or a safety strap attached to the harness or collar. Whatever you do, do not let your dog ride in the back of a pickup truck unless he is securely tied on a very short lead.

I've seen trucks stop quickly and, even though the dog was tied, it fell out and was dragged.

I do occasionally let my dogs ride loose with me because I really enjoy their

Consider the temperature when traveling with your Westie. This pup has figured out an innovative way to beat the heat.

The Nylabone® Fold-Away Pet Carrier is easy to assemble, making traveling with your pet easier.

companionship, but in all honesty they are safer in their crates. I have a friend whose van rolled in an accident but his dogs, in their fiberglass crates, were not injured nor did they escape.

Another advantage of the crate is that it is a safe place to leave him if you need to run into the store. Otherwise you wouldn't be able to leave the windows down. Keep in mind that while many dogs are overly protective in their crates, this may not be enough to deter dognappers. In some states it is against the law to leave a dog in the car unattended.

Never leave a dog loose in the car wearing a collar and leash. I have known more than one dog that has killed himself by hanging. Do not let him put his head out an open window. Foreign debris can be blown into his eyes. When leaving your dog unattended in a car, consider the temperature. It can take less than five minutes to reach temperatures over 100 degrees Fahrenheit.

TRIPS

Perhaps you are taking a trip. Give consideration to what is best for your dog–traveling with you or boarding. When

The Nylabone® Fold-Away Pet Carrier is light-weight and easy to carry.

traveling by car, van or motor home, you need to think ahead about locking your vehicle. In all probability you have many valuables in the car and do not wish to leave it unlocked. Perhaps most valuable and not replaceable is your dog. Give thought to securing your vehicle and providing adequate ventilation for him. Another consideration for you when traveling with your dog is medical problems that may arise and little inconveniences, such as exposure to external parasites. Some areas of the country are quite flea infested. You may want to carry flea spray with you. This is even a good idea when staying in motels. Quite possibly you are not the only occupant of the room.

Unbelievably many motels and even hotels do allow canine guests, even some very first-class ones. Gaines Pet Foods Corporation publishes *Touring With Towser*, a directory of domestic hotels and motels that accommodate guests with dogs. Their address is 585 Hawthorne Court, Galesburg, IL, 61401. I would recommend you call ahead to any motel that you may be considering and see if they accept pets. Sometimes it is necessary to pay a deposit against room damage. Of course you are more likely to gain accommodations for a small dog than a large dog. Also the management feels reassured when you mention that your dog will be crated. Since my dogs tend to bark when I leave the room, I leave the TV on nearly full blast to deaden the noises outside that tend to encourage my dogs to bark. If you do travel with your dog, take along plenty of baggies so that you can clean up after him. When we all do our share in cleaning up, we make it possible for motels to continue accepting our pets. As a matter of fact, you should practice cleaning up everywhere you take your dog.

Westies can make themselves at home anywhere they go—just make sure in advance that the places you are visiting welcome pets.

Depending on where your are traveling, you may need an up-to-date health certificate issued by your veterinarian. It is good policy to take along your dog's medical information, which would include the name, address and phone number of your veterinarian, vaccination record, rabies certificate, and any medication he is taking.

AIR TRAVEL

When traveling by air, you need to contact the airlines to check their policy. Usually you have to make arrangements up to a couple of weeks in advance for traveling with your dog. The airlines require your dog to travel in an airline approved fiberglass crate. Usually these can be purchased through the airlines but they are also readily available in most pet-supply stores. If your dog is not accustomed to a crate, then it is a

good idea to get him acclimated to it before your trip. The day of the actual trip you should withhold water about one hour ahead of departure and no food for about 12 hours. The airlines generally have temperature restrictions, which do not allow pets to travel if it is either too cold or too hot. Frequently these restrictions are based on the temperatures at the departure and arrival airports. It's best to inquire about a health certificate. These usually need to be issued within ten days of departure. You should arrange for non-stop, direct flights and if a commuter plane should be involved, check to see if it will carry dogs. Some don't. The Humane Society of the United States has put together a tip sheet for airline traveling. You can receive a copy by sending a self-addressed stamped envelope to:

Keeping your dog on a leash will prevent him from becoming separated from you in a strange place. An extra precaution is a collar with identification tags.

The Humane Society of the United States

Tip Sheet
2100 L Street NW
Washington, DC 20037.

Regulations differ for traveling outside of the country and are sometimes changed without notice. Well in advance you need to write or call the appropriate consulate or agricultural department for instructions. Some countries have lengthy quarantines (six months), and countries differ in their rabies vaccination requirements. For instance, it may have to be given at least 30 days ahead of your departure.

Do make sure your dog is wearing proper identification.

Many Westies will learn to like traveling—but to this extent? McGregor, owned by Bob and Winnie Napoli, is dressed and ready to hop on his motorcycle and ride into the sunset.

You never know when you might be in an accident and separated from your dog. Or your dog could be frightened and somehow manage to escape and run away. When I travel, my dogs wear collars with engraved nameplates with my name, phone number and city.

Another suggestion would be to carry in-case-of-emergency instructions. These would include the address and phone number of a relative or friend, your veterinarian's name, address and phone number, and your dog's medical information.

"We want to come, too!" Exercise pens are portable and can be easily taken along to give your Westie a safe place to play once you reach your destination.

BOARDING KENNELS

Perhaps you have decided that you need to board your dog. Your veterinarian can recommend a good boarding facility or possibly a pet sitter that will come to your house. It is customary for the boarding kennel to ask for proof of vaccination for the DHLPP, rabies and bordetella vaccine. The bordetella should have been given within six months of boarding. This is for your protection. If they do not ask for this proof I would not board at their kennel. Ask about flea control. Those dogs that suffer flea-bite allergy can get in trouble at a boarding kennel. Unfortunately boarding kennels are limited on how much they are able to do.

For more information on pet sitting, contact NAPPS:
National Association of Professional Pet Sitters
6 State Road
Suite 113
Mechanicsburg, PA 17050

Our clinic has technicians that pet sit and technicians that board clinic patients in their homes. This may be an alternative for you. Ask your veterinarian if they have an employee that can help you. There is a definite advantage of having a technician care for your dog, especially if your dog is on medication or is a senior citizen.

You can write for a copy of *Traveling With Your Pet* from ASPCA, Education Department, 441 E. 92nd Street, New York, NY 10028.

A reputable boarding kennel will require that dogs receive the vaccination for kennel cough no less than two weeks before their scheduled stay.

BEHAVIOR and Canine Communication

Studies of the human/animal bond point out the importance of the unique relationships that exist between people and their pets. Those of us who share our lives with pets understand the special part they play through companionship, service and protection.

Senior citizens show more concern for their own eating habits when they have the responsibility of feeding a dog. Seeing that their dog is routinely exercised encourages the owner to think of schedules that otherwise may seem unimportant to the senior citizen. The older owner may be arthritic and feeling poorly but with

The bond between humans and dogs is a powerful one. A visit from a Westie can have a therapeutic effect on hospital patients and senior citizens.

responsibility for his dog he has a reason to get up and get moving. It is a big plus if his dog is an attention seeker who will demand such from his owner.

Over the last couple of decades, it has been shown that pets relieve the stress of those who lead busy lives. Owning a pet has been known to lessen the occurrence of heart attack and stroke.

Many single folks thrive on the companionship of a dog. Lifestyles are very different from a long time ago, and today more individuals seek the single life. However, they receive fulfillment from owning a dog.

Most likely the majority of our dogs live in family environments. The companionship they provide is well worth the effort involved. In my opinion, every child should have the opportunity to have a family dog. Dogs teach responsibility through understanding their care, feelings and even respecting their life cycles. Frequently those children who have not been exposed to dogs grow up afraid of dogs, which isn't good. Dogs sense timidity and some will take advantage of the situation.

A Westie makes a great addition to any household. Floyd rests in his favorite spot on the stairs.

Today more dogs are serving as service dogs. Since the origination of the Seeing Eye dogs years ago, we now have trained hearing dogs. Also dogs are trained to provide service for the handicapped and are able to perform many different tasks for their owners. Search and Rescue dogs, with their handlers, are sent throughout the world to assist in recovery of disaster victims. They are life savers.

Therapy dogs are very popular with nursing homes, and some hospitals even allow them to visit. The inhabitants truly look forward to their visits. I have taken a couple of my dogs visiting and left in tears when I saw the response of the patients. They wanted and were allowed to have my dogs in their beds to hold and love.

Nationally there is a Pet Awareness Week to educate students and others about the value and basic care of our pets. Many countries take an even greater interest in their pets than

Americans do. In those countries the pets are allowed to accompany their owners into restaurants and shops, etc. In the U.S. this freedom is only available to our service dogs. Even so we think very highly of the human/animal bond.

CANINE BEHAVIOR

Canine behavior problems are the number-one reason for pet owners to dispose of their dogs, either through new homes, humane shelters or euthanasia. Unfortunately there are too many owners who are unwilling to devote the necessary time to properly train their dogs. On the other hand, there are those who not only are concerned about inherited health problems but are also aware of the dog's mental stability.

You may realize that a breed and his group relatives (i.e., sporting, hounds, etc.) show tendencies to behavioral characteristics. An experienced breeder can acquaint you with his breed's personality. Unfortunately many breeds are labeled with poor temperaments when actually the breed as a whole is not affected but only a small percentage of individuals within the breed.

If the breed in question is very popular, then of course there may be a higher number of unstable dogs. Do not label a breed good or bad. I know of absolutely awful-tempered dogs within one of our most popular, lovable breeds.

Inheritance and environment contribute to the dog's behavior. Some naïve people suggest inbreeding as the cause of bad temperaments. Inbreeding only results in poor behavior if the ancestors carry the trait. If there are excellent temperaments behind the dogs, then inbreeding will promote good temperaments in the offspring. Did you ever consider that inbreeding is what sets the characteristics of a breed? A purebred dog is the end result of inbreeding. This does not spare the mixed-breed dog from the same problems. Mixed-breed dogs frequently are the offspring of purebred dogs.

When planning a breeding, I like to observe the potential stud and his offspring in the show ring. If I see unruly behavior, I try to look into it further. I want to know if it is genetic or environmental, due to the lack of training and socialization. A good breeder will avoid breeding mentally unsound dogs.

Not too many decades ago most of our dogs led a different

lifestyle than what is prevalent today. Usually mom stayed home so the dog had human companionship and someone to discipline it if needed. Not much was expected from the dog. Today's mom works and everyone's life is at a much faster pace.

The dog may have to adjust to being a "weekend" dog. The family is gone all day during the week, and the dog is left to his own devices for entertainment. Some dogs sleep all day waiting for their family to come home and others become wigwam wreckers if given the opportunity. Crates do ensure the safety of the dog and the house. However, he could become a physically and emotionally cripple if he doesn't get enough exercise and attention. We still appreciate and want the companionship of our dogs although we expect more from them. In many cases we tend to forget dogs are just that—*dogs* not human beings.

Members of the same breed share many of the same characteristics. Certain aspects of a dog's temperament are inherited.

I own several dogs who are left crated during the day but I do try to make time for them in the evenings and on the weekends. Also we try to do something together before I leave for work. Maybe it

helps them to have the companionship of other dogs. They accept their crates as their personal "houses" and seem to be content with their routine and thrive on trying their best to please me.

SOCIALIZING AND TRAINING

Many prospective puppy buyers lack experience regarding the proper socialization and training needed to develop the type of pet we all desire. In the first 18 months, training does take some work. Trust me, it is easier to start proper training before there is a problem that needs to be corrected.

The initial work begins with the breeder. The breeder should start socializing the puppy at five to six weeks of age and cannot let up. Human socializing is critical up through 12 weeks of age and likewise important during the following months. The litter should be left together during the first few weeks but it is necessary to separate them by ten weeks of age. Leaving them together after that time will increase competition for litter dominance. If puppies are not socialized with people by 12 weeks of age, they will be timid in later life.

The eight- to ten-week age period is a fearful time for puppies. They need to be handled very gently around children and adults. There should be no harsh discipline during this time. Starting at 14 weeks of age, the puppy begins the juvenile period, which ends when he reaches sexual maturity around six to 14 months of age. During the juvenile period he needs to be introduced to strangers (adults, children and other dogs) on the home property. At sexual maturity he will begin to bark at strangers and become more protective. Males start to lift their legs to urinate but if you desire you can inhibit this

Well-socialized pups should be able to play with their littermates and other puppies without showing aggression.

behavior by walking your boy on leash away from trees, shrubs, fences, etc.

Perhaps you are thinking about an older puppy. You need to inquire about the puppy's social experience. If he has lived in a kennel, he may have a hard time adjusting to people and environmental stimuli. Assuming he has had a good social upbringing, there are advantages to an older puppy.

Training includes puppy kindergarten

Puppies' first weeks are critical because the socialization they receive when they are young will shape their behavior throughout their lives.

Pups should be left together for their first few weeks, but should be separated by ten weeks of age.

and a minimum of one to two basic training classes. During these classes you will learn how to dominate your youngster. This is especially important if you own a large breed of dog. It is somewhat harder, if not nearly

impossible, for some owners to be the Alpha figure when their dog towers over them. You will be taught how to properly restrain your dog. This concept is important. Again it puts you in the Alpha position. All dogs need to be restrained many times during their lives. Believe it or not, some of our worst offenders are the eight-week-old puppies that are brought to our clinic. They need to be gently restrained for a nail trim but the way they carry on you would think we were killing them. In comparison, their vaccination is a "piece of cake." When we ask dogs to do something that is not agreeable to them, then their worst comes out. Life will be easier for your dog if you expose him at a young age to the necessities of life—proper behavior and restraint.

UNDERSTANDING THE DOG'S LANGUAGE

Most authorities agree that the dog is a descendent of the wolf. The dog and wolf have similar traits. For instance both are pack oriented and prefer not to be isolated for long periods of time. Another characteristic is that the dog, like the wolf, looks to the leader—Alpha—for direction. Both the wolf and the dog communicate through body language, not only within their pack but with outsiders.

Every pack has an Alpha figure. The dog looks to you, or should look to you, to be that leader. If your dog doesn't receive the proper training and guidance, he very well may replace you as Alpha. This would be a serious problem and is certainly a disservice to your dog.

Eye contact is one way the Alpha wolf keeps order within his pack. You are Alpha so you must establish eye contact with your puppy. Obviously your puppy will have to look at you. Practice eye contact even if you need to hold his head for five to ten seconds at a time. You can give him a treat as a reward. Make sure your eye contact is gentle and not threatening. Later, if he has been naughty, it is permissible to give him a long, penetrating look. I caution you there are some older dogs that never learned eye contact as puppies and cannot accept eye contact. You should avoid eye contact with these dogs since they feel threatened and will retaliate as such.

BODY LANGUAGE

The play bow, when the forequarters are down and the

hindquarters are elevated, is an invitation to play. Puppies play fight, which helps them learn the acceptable limits of biting. This is necessary for later in their lives. Nevertheless, an owner may be falsely reassured by the playful nature of his dog's aggression. Playful aggression toward another dog or human may be an indication of serious aggression in the future. Owners should never play fight or play tug-of-war with any dog that is inclined to be dominant.

Signs of submission are:

1. Avoids eye contact.

2. Active submission—the dog crouches down, ears back and the tail is lowered.

3. Passive submission—the dog rolls on his side with his hindlegs in the air and frequently urinates.

There's a dominant personality in every bunch—one or two pups will remain "on top" of every situation. Notice the "color coding" on the puppies' backs.

Signs of dominance are:

1. Makes eye contact.

2. Stands with ears up, tail up and the hair raised on his neck.

3. Shows dominance over another dog by standing at right angles over it.

Dominant dogs tend to behave in characteristic ways such as:

1. The dog may be unwilling to move from his place (i.e., reluctant to give up the sofa if the owner wants to sit there).

2. He may not part with toys or objects in his mouth and may show possessiveness with his food bowl.

3. He may not respond quickly to commands.

4. He may be disagreeable for grooming and dislikes to be petted.

Dogs are popular because of their sociable nature. Those

that have contact with humans during the first 12 weeks of life regard them as a member of their own species—their pack. All dogs have the potential for both dominant and submissive behavior. Only through experience and training do they learn to whom it is appropriate to show which behavior. Not all dogs are concerned with dominance but owners need to be aware of that potential. It is wise for the owner to establish his dominance early on.

A human can express dominance or submission toward a dog in the following ways:

1. Meeting the dog's gaze signals dominance. Averting the gaze signals submission. If the dog growls or threatens, averting the gaze is the first avoiding action to take—it may prevent attack. It is important to establish eye contact in the puppy. The older dog that has not been exposed to eye contact may see it as a threat and will not be willing to submit.

2. Being taller than the dog signals dominance; being lower signals submission. This is why, when attempting to make friends with a strange dog or catch the runaway, one should kneel down to his level. Some owners see their dogs become dominant when allowed on the furniture or on the bed. Then he is at the owner's level.

3. An owner can gain dominance by ignoring all the dog's social initiatives. The owner pays attention to the dog only when he obeys a command.

No dog should be allowed to achieve dominant status over any adult or child. Ways of preventing are as follows:

1. Handle the puppy gently, especially during the three- to four-month period.

Being above your dog and making eye contact are ways to signal your dominance. Make eye contact with your Westie when he is a pup so he does not perceive you as a threat.

2. Let the children and adults handfeed him and teach him to take food without lunging or grabbing.
3. Do not allow him to chase children or joggers.
4. Do not allow him to jump on people or mount their legs. Even females may be inclined to mount. It is not only a male habit.
5. Do not allow him to growl for any reason.
6. Don't participate in wrestling or tug-of-war games.
7. Don't physically punish puppies for aggressive behavior. Restrain him from repeating the infraction and teach an alternative behavior. Dogs should earn everything they receive from their owners. This would include sitting to receive petting or treats, sitting before going out the door and sitting to receive the collar and leash. These types of exercises reinforce the owner's dominance.

Teach your Westie how you want him to behave—having him sit to receive treats, to be petted, and to have his collar and leash put on will further reinforce your dominance.

Young children should never be left alone with a dog. It is important that children learn some basic obedience commands so they have some control over the dog. They will gain the respect of their dog.

FEAR

One of the most common problems dogs experience is being fearful. Some dogs are more afraid than others. On the lesser side, which is sometimes humorous to watch, my dog can be afraid of a strange object. He acts silly when something is out of place in the house. I call his problem perceptive intelligence. He realizes the abnormal within his known environment. He does not react the same way in strange environments since he does not know what is normal.

On the more serious side is a fear of people. This can result in backing off, seeking his own space and saying "leave me alone" or it can result in an aggressive behavior that may lead

McGregor's not fearful—he has all kinds of friends!

to challenging the person. Respect that the dog wants to be left alone and give him time to come forward. If you approach the cornered dog, he may resort to snapping. If you leave him alone, he may decide to come forward, which should be rewarded with a treat. Years ago we had a dog that behaved in this manner. We coaxed people to stop by the house and make friends with our fearful dog. She learned to take the treats and after weeks of work she overcame her suspicions and made friends more readily.

Some dogs may initially be too fearful to take treats. In these cases it is helpful to make sure the dog hasn't eaten for about 24 hours. Being a little hungry encourages him to accept the treats, especially if they are of the "gourmet" variety. I have a dog that worries about strangers since people seldom stop by my house. Over the years she has learned a cue and jumps up quickly to visit anyone sitting on the sofa. She learned by herself that all guests on the sofa were to be trusted friends. I think she felt more comfortable with them being at her level, rather than towering over her.

Dogs can be afraid of numerous things, including loud noises and thunderstorms. Invariably the owner rewards (by comforting) the dog when it shows signs of fearfulness. I had a terrible problem with my favorite dog in the Utility obedience class. Not only was he intimidated in the class but he was afraid of noise and afraid of displeasing me. Frequently he would knock down the bar jump, which clattered dreadfully. I gave him credit because he continued to try to clear it, although he was terribly scared. I finally learned to "reward" him every time he knocked down the jump. I would jump up and down, clap my hands and tell him how great he was. My psychology worked, he relaxed and eventually cleared the jump with ease. When your dog is frightened, direct his attention to something else and act happy. Don't dwell on his fright.

Fear can make some Westies just want to hide!

AGGRESSION

Some different types of aggression are: predatory, defensive, dominance, possessive, protective, fear induced, noise provoked, "rage" syndrome (unprovoked aggression), maternal and aggression directed toward other dogs. Aggression is the most common behavioral problem encountered. Protective breeds are expected to be more aggressive than others but with the proper upbringing they can make very dependable companions. You need to be able to read your dog.

Many factors contribute to aggression including genetics and environment. An improper environment, which may include the living conditions, lack of social life, excessive punishment, being attacked or frightened by an aggressive dog, etc., can all influence a dog's behavior. Even spoiling him and giving too much praise may be detrimental. Isolation and the lack of human contact or exposure to frequent teasing by children or adults also can ruin a good dog. Lack of direction, fear, or confusion lead to aggression in those dogs that are so inclined. Any obedience exercise, even the sit and down, can direct the dog and overcome fear and/or confusion. Every dog should learn these commands as a youngster, and there should be periodic reinforcement.

When a dog is showing signs of aggression, you should speak calmly (no screaming or hysterics) and firmly give a command that he understands, such as the sit. As soon as your dog obeys, you have assumed your dominant position. Aggression presents a problem because there may be danger to others. Sometimes it is an emotional issue. Owners may consciously or unconsciously encourage their dog's aggression. Other owners show responsibility by accepting the problem and taking measures to keep it under control. The owner is responsible for his dog's actions, and it is not wise to take a chance on someone being bitten, especially a child. Euthanasia is the solution for some owners and in severe cases this may be the best choice. However, few dogs are that dangerous and very few are that much of a threat to their owners. If caution is exercised and professional help is gained early on, then I surmise most cases can be controlled.

Some authorities recommend feeding a lower protein (less than 20 percent) diet. They believe this can aid in reducing aggression. If the dog loses weight, then vegetable oil can be added. Veterinarians and behaviorists are having some success with pharmacology. In many cases treatment is possible and can improve the situation.

If you have done everything according to "the book" regarding training and socializing and are still having a behavior problem, don't procrastinate. It is important that the problem gets attention before it is out of hand. It is estimated that 20 percent of a veterinarian's time may be devoted to dealing with problems before they become so intolerable that the dog is separated from its home and owner. If your veterinarian isn't able to help, he should refer you to a behaviorist.

Barking

This is a habit that shouldn't be encouraged. Over the years I've had new puppy owners call to say that their dog hasn't learned to bark. I assure them they are indeed fortunate but not to worry. Some owners desire their dog to bark so as to be a watchdog. In my experience, most dogs will bark when a stranger comes to the door.

The new puppy frequently barks or whines in the crate in his strange environment and the owner reinforces the puppy's bad behavior by going to him during the night. This is a no-no. I tell my new owners to smack the top of the crate and say "quiet" in a loud, firm voice. The puppies don't like to hear the loud

A stable environment where pups are well taken care of and given room to run and play will positively affect their temperaments as they develop.

noise of the crate being banged. If the barking is sleep-interrupting, then the owner should take crate and pup to the bedroom for a few days until the puppy becomes adjusted to his new environment. Otherwise ignore the barking during the night.

Barking can be an inherited problem or a bad habit learned through the environment. It takes dedication to stop the barking. Attention should be paid to the cause of the barking. Does the dog seek attention, does he need to go out, is it feeding time, is it occurring when he is left alone, is it a protective bark, etc.? Presently I have a ten-week-old puppy that is a real loud mouth, which I am sure is an inherited tendency. Both her mother and especially her grandmother are overzealous barkers but fortunately have mellowed with the years. My young puppy is corrected with a firm "no" and gentle shaking and she is responding. When barking presents a problem for you, try to stop it as soon as it begins.

Westies are known for being intelligent, but intellectual? This young Westie is sniffing around for some new reading material.

There are electronic collars available that are supposed to curb barking. Personally I have not had experience with them. There are some disadvantages to to the collar. If the dog is barking out of excitement, punishment is not the appropriate treatment. Presumably there is the chance the collar could be activated by other stimuli and thereby punish the dog when it is not barking. Should you decide to use one, then you should seek help from a person with experience with that type of collar. In my opinion I feel the root of the problem needs to be investigated and corrected.

In extreme circumstances (usually when there is a problem with the neighbors), some people have resorted to having their

Your Westie may jump up as a sign of affection or just to say hello, but if it is a behavior you wish to discourage you should do so right from the start.

dogs debarked. I caution you that the dog continues to bark but usually only a squeaking sound is heard. Frequently the vocal cords grow back. Probably the biggest concern is that the dog can be left with scar tissue which can narrow the opening to the trachea.

Jumping Up

Personally, I am not thrilled when other dogs jump on me but I have hurt feelings if they don't! I do encourage my own dogs to jump on me, on command. Some do and some don't. In my opinion, a dog that jumps up is a happy dog. Nevertheless few guests appreciate dogs jumping on them. Clothes get footprinted and/or snagged.

I am a believer in allowing the puppy to jump up during his first few weeks. In my opinion if you correct him too soon and at the wrong age you may intimidate him. Consequently he could be timid around humans later in his life. However, there will come a time, probably around four months of age, that he needs to know when it is okay to jump and when he is to show off good manners by sitting instead.

Some authorities never allow jumping. If you are irritated by your dog jumping up on you, then you should discourage it from the beginning. A larger breed of dog can cause harm to a senior citizen. Some are quite fragile. It may not take much to cause a topple that could break a hip.

How do you correct the problem? All family members need to participate in teaching the puppy to sit as soon as he starts to jump up. The sit must be practiced every time he starts to jump up. Don't forget to praise him for his good behavior. If an older dog has acquired the habit, grasp his paws and squeeze tightly. Give a firm "No." He'll soon catch on. Remember the entire family must take part. Each time you allow him to jump up you go back a step in training.

Biting

All puppies bite and try to chew on your fingers, toes, arms, etc. This is the time to teach them to be gentle and not bite hard. Put your fingers in your puppy's mouth and if he bites too hard then say "easy" and let him know he's hurting you. I squeal and act like I have been seriously hurt. If the puppy plays too rough and doesn't respond to your corrections, then he needs "Time Out" in his crate. You should be particularly careful with young children and puppies who still have their deciduous (baby) teeth. Those teeth are like needles and can leave little scars on youngsters. My adult daughter still has a small scar on her face from when she teased an eight-week-old puppy as an eight-year-old.

Biting in the more mature dog is something that should be prevented at all costs. Should it occur I would quickly let him know in no uncertain terms that biting will not be tolerated. When biting is directed toward another dog (dog fight), don't get in the middle of it. On more than one occasion I have had to separate a couple of my dogs and usually was in the middle of that one last lunge by the offender. Some authorities recommend breaking up a fight by elevating the hind legs. This would only be possible if there was a person for each dog.

Obviously it would be hard to fight with the hind legs off the ground. A dog bite is serious and should be given attention. Wash the bite with soap and water and contact your doctor. It is important to know the status of the offender's rabies vaccination.

I have several dogs that are sensitive to having mats combed out of their coats and eventually they have had enough. They give fair warning by turning and acting like they would like to nip my offending fingers. However, one verbal warning from me says, "I'm sorry, don't you dare think about biting me and please let me carefully comb just a little bit more." I have owned a minimum of 30 dogs and raised many more puppies and have yet to have one of my dogs bite me except during that last lunge in the two or three dog fights I felt compelled to break up. My dogs wouldn't dare bite me. They know who is boss.

You never know what even the most innocent-looking Westie pup will stick his nose into next.

This is not always the case for other owners. I do not wish to frighten you but when biting occurs you should seek professional help at once. On the other hand you must not let your dog intimidate you and be so afraid of a bite that you can't discipline him. Professional help through your veterinarian, dog trainer and/or behaviorist can give you guidance.

Mischief and Misbehavior

All puppies and even some adult dogs will get into mischief at some time in their lives. You should start by "puppy proofing" your house. Even so it is impossible to have a sterile environment. For instance, if you would be down to four walls and a floor your dog could still chew a hole in the wall. What do you do? Remember puppies should never be left unsupervised so let us go on to the trusted adult dog that has misbehaved. His behavior may be an attention getter. Dogs, and even children, are known to do mischief even though they know they will be punished. Your puppy/dog will benefit from more attention and new direction. He may benefit from a training class or by reinforcing the obedience he has already learned. How about a daily walk? That could be a good outlet for your dog, time together and exercise for both of you.

My most important advice to you is to be aware of your dog's actions. Even so, remember dogs are dogs and will behave as such even though we might like them to be perfect little people. You and your dog will become neurotic if you worry about every little indiscretion. When there is reason for concern—don't waste time. Seek guidance. Dogs are meant to be loved and enjoyed.

References:

Manual of Canine Behavior, Valerie O'Farrell, British Small Animal Veterinary Association.

Good Owners, Great Dogs, Brian Kilcommons, Warner Books.

Naturally inquisitive Westie puppies are bound to find mischief. Punishment isn't always the answer—let your pup be a pup and enjoy his amusing antics!

RESOURCES

American Kennel Club
Headquarters:
260 Madison Avenue
New York, NY 10016

Operations Center:
5580 Centerview Drive
Raleigh, NC 27606-3390

Customer Services:
Phone: 919-233-9767
Fax: 919-816-3627
www.akc.org

The Kennel Club
1 Clarges Street
Picadilly, London WIY
8AB, England
www.the-kennel-club.org.uk

The Canadian Kennel Club
89 Skyway Avenue
Suite 100
Etobicoke, Ontario,
Canada M9W 6R4
www.ckc.ca

The United Kennel Club, Inc.
100 E. Kilgore Road
Kalamazoo, MI 49002-5584
616-343-9020
www.ukcdogs.com

INDEX